T0328605

Cambridge Elements ═

Elements in the Philosophy of Immanuel Kant
edited by
Desmond Hogan
Princeton University
Howard Williams
University of Cardiff
Allen Wood
Indiana University

KANT ON FREEDOM

Owen Ware
University of Toronto

CAMBRIDGE
UNIVERSITY PRESS

Shaftesbury Road, Cambridge CB2 8EA, United Kingdom

One Liberty Plaza, 20th Floor, New York, NY 10006, USA

477 Williamstown Road, Port Melbourne, VIC 3207, Australia

314–321, 3rd Floor, Plot 3, Splendor Forum, Jasola District Centre, New Delhi – 110025, India

103 Penang Road, #05–06/07, Visioncrest Commercial, Singapore 238467

Cambridge University Press is part of Cambridge University Press & Assessment, a department of the University of Cambridge.

We share the University's mission to contribute to society through the pursuit of education, learning and research at the highest international levels of excellence.

www.cambridge.org
Information on this title: www.cambridge.org/9781009074551

DOI: 10.1017/9781009070652

First published 2023

A catalogue record for this publication is available from the British Library.

ISBN 978-1-009-07455-1 Paperback
ISSN 2397-9461 (online)
ISSN 2514-3824 (print)

Cambridge University Press & Assessment has no responsibility for the persistence or accuracy of URLs for external or third-party internet websites referred to in this publication and does not guarantee that any content on such websites is, or will remain, accurate or appropriate.

Kant on Freedom

Elements in the Philosophy of Immanuel Kant

DOI: 10.1017/9781009070652
First published online: May 2023

Owen Ware
University of Toronto
Author for correspondence: Owen Ware, Owen.ware@utoronto.ca

Abstract: Kant's early critics maintained that his theory of freedom faces a dilemma: either it reduces the will's activity to strict necessity by making it subject to the causality of the moral law, or it reduces the will's activity to blind chance by liberating it from rules of any kind. This Element offers a new interpretation of Kant's theory against the backdrop of this controversy. It argues that Kant was a consistent proponent of the claim that the moral law is the causal law of a free will, and that the supposed ability of free will to choose indifferently between options is an empty concept. Freedom, for Kant, is a power to initiate action from oneself, and the only way to exercise this power is through the law of one's own will, the moral law. Immoral action is not thereby rendered impossible, but it also does not express a genuine ability.

Keywords: freedom, choice, determinism, morality, evil

ISBNs: 9781009074551 (PB), 9781009070652 (OC)
ISSNs: 2397-9461 (online), 2514-3824 (print)

Contents

1 Introduction: The Free Will Dilemma 1

2 Kant's Moral Necessitarianism: Against Indifference 6

3 The Reception of Kant's Theory of Freedom 28

4 Concluding Remarks 40

Appendix A: Moral Progress and Perfection 44

Appendix B: Timeline of the Freedom Controversy 47

List of Abbreviations 48

References 49

Since the free choice of God and the good angels cannot sin, "the ability to sin"
does not belong in the definition of freedom of choice.

—ANSELM

In order to be free, there is no need for me to be inclined in both ways.

—DESCARTES

Freedom of indifference is a nonentity

—KANT[1]

1 Introduction: The Free Will Dilemma

In recent years, scholars have become increasingly interested in the development of Kant's theory of freedom from the *Critique of Pure Reason*, first
published in 1781, to his last major work in practical philosophy, the 1797
Metaphysics of Morals.[2] What has struck commentators as odd is that Kant's
thinking about freedom seems to have gone through three phases during this
time. In the first phase, which includes the *Groundwork for the Metaphysics of
Morals* (1785) and the *Critique of Practical Reason* (1788), he seems committed to a form of *moral necessitarianism*, according to which the moral law is the
necessary causal law of a free will. Kant seems to abandon this position in favor
of moral libertarianism in his 1792 essay "On the Radical Evil of Human
Nature" (later incorporated into the *Religion* of 1793), according to which
freedom is the capacity to choose for or against the moral law. In the third and
final phase, however, Kant appears to revert to his original stance, arguing that
"freedom of choice cannot be defined – as some have tried to define it – as the
ability to make a choice for or against the law" (MS, AA 6:226).[3]

This timeline invites the question of why Kant appears to have embraced
a liberty of indifference view in 1792, whereas both *before* and *after* that date he
was a vocal critic of the view. As several scholars have come to see, the answer
to this question lies in a debate that surrounded Kant's theory of freedom in the
late 1780s and 1790s, which I shall call the *Freiheitsstreit* (freedom

---

[1] Anselm (1080–1086) 2007, chap. 1; Descartes (1641) 1996, 40; V-Met/Mron, AA 29:901.
[2] See Wood 1984; Allison 1990, 2020; Korsgaard 1996; Timmermann 2003; Watkins 2004;
Pereboom 2006; Engstrom 2009; Guyer 2009, 2017; McCarty 2009; Hogan 2009a, 2009b;
Stern 2011; Ameriks 2012; Insole 2013; Frierson 2014; Dunn 2015; Kohl 2015a, 2015b;
Papish 2018; McClear 2020; Kain 2021; Ware 2023; Schafer, forthcoming.
[3] "Die Freiheit der Willkür aber kann nicht durch das Vermögen der Wahl, für oder wider das
Gesetz zu handeln, (*libertas indifferentiae*) definirt werden – wie es wohl einige versucht haben."
Compare with Kant's preparatory work for the Preface and Introduction to the *Metaphysics of
Morals*, especially the fragment labelled *Loses Blatt E 36*: "But this freedom cannot be explained
as the subjective possibility [of acting] according to the law or against it, i.e., to settle upon the
unlawfulness of actions in general, because that would count as an evil will. That would draw
sensibility into the field of pure reason" (VAMS, AA 24:248).

controversy).[4] The controversy was set in motion when Johann August Heinrich Ulrich (1746–1813), a professor of philosophy at the University of Jena, published *Eleutheriology, or Concerning Freedom and Necessity* (1788). In this book Ulrich claims that although Kant saves freedom from phenomenal determinism, he reintroduces the problem at the noumenal level by making the moral law the causal law of a free will.[5] His claim is that Kant's moral necessitarianism exposed him to the following objection, which I will call the *Objection from Necessity*:

> *Objection from Necessity.* If we define the moral law as the causal law of a free will, then we lose the grounds on which to explain how the will is genuinely free in its activity. We rescue the will from determinism at the phenomenal level, only to reintroduce the problem at the noumenal level, making the will subject to a kind of intelligible fatalism which undermines the idea of freedom itself.

Before Kant's essay on evil appeared, Karl Leonard Reinhold (1757–1823) published his *Attempt at a New Theory of the Human Power of Representation* (1789), in which he advances a friendly amendment to Kant's definition of freedom. Like Ulrich, Reinhold was troubled by the appearance of noumenal determinism surrounding Kant's theory of freedom. But unlike Ulrich, he thought that the spirit of Kant's theory required a modified definition of the will as a capacity to choose for or against the moral law. Accordingly, Reinhold proposes this amendment on Kant's behalf in order to provide a more charitable view of his position. From Reinhold's perspective, the fact that Kant seemed to accept liberty of indifference in his 1792 essay was news he was happy to accept. After all, Kant's modified account seems to allow for the will's freedom to choose between a good and an evil character, along the lines Reinhold had proposed.

But Kant's critics were not satisfied with his 1792 essay either, for reasons that soon became clear in a publication by Christoph Andreas Leonhard Creuzer (1768–1844) titled *Skeptical Observations on the Freedom of the Will* (1793). Creuzer's objection was that by defining freedom of will as the capacity to choose for or against the moral law in the adoption of one's character, Kant

---

4 See Fabbianelli 2015; Gardner 2017; Guyer 2017; Noller 2019; Smith 2021. I have coined the expression *Freiheitsstreit* here to distinguish the free will debate from the roughly contemporaneous *Pantheismusstreit* (pantheism controversy) and *Atheismusstreit* (atheism controversy). See Appendix B for a timeline.

5 The same view was later affirmed by one of Ulrich's younger colleagues in Jena, Carl Christian Erhard Schmid (1762–1812), who argues in his *Attempt at a Moral Philosophy* ([1790] 1792) that Kant turns freedom of the will into a kind of "intelligible fatalism." While the phrase "intelligible fatalism" would quickly become a point of criticism against Kant, Schmid himself was an advocate of this view.

rescues freedom from the snares of noumenal necessity only to subject it to something equally destructive of it – noumenal chance. The moment Kant alters his position to make room for liberty of indifference between a good and evil character, he undercuts the ground on which to explain why one chooses to act one way rather than the other. As a result, Creuzer concludes, Kant's moral libertarianism exposes him to a new objection, which I will call the *Objection from Chance*:

> *Objection from Chance*. If we define the will in terms of liberty of indifference, the capacity to choose for or against the moral law, then we lose the grounds on which to explain why the will acts one way rather than the other. We thereby rescue the will from determinism, only to reduce its activity to mere chance at the noumenal level, which also undermines the idea of freedom.[6]

By the early 1790s, then, the *Freiheitsstreit* had taken the expanded form of a dilemma, which we may summarize as follows:

The Free Will Dilemma
First Horn

(1) The moral law is the necessary causal law of a free will.
(2) A will subject to the causality of the moral law is determined.
(3) Therefore, a moral will's activity reduces to necessity.

Second Horn

(1) A will must be free to choose its character, either good or evil.
(2) There is no explanation for the ground of this choice.
(3) Therefore, the will's choice of character reduces to mere chance.

With the benefit of hindsight, this timeline of events making up the *Freiheitsstreit* appears to explain an otherwise perplexing series of shifts in Kant's mature theory of freedom. Wanting to avoid the Objection from Necessity leveled by Ulrich, Kant seems to embrace a form of moral libertarianism according to which one has the power to choose for or against the moral law. Yet when he finds himself exposed to the Objection from Chance leveled by

---

[6] The roots of this objection date as far back as the Stoics, who thought that the Epicurean "swerve" reduced freedom to blind chance. In Kant's day, the worry surfaced in the context of Crusius's account of freedom. Today, versions of the Objection from Chance have been consistently leveled against theories of libertarian freedom (often under the name of the Luck Objection or Randomness Objection). See Pereboom 2001; Fischer 2011; Franklin 2011; Tognazzini 2015; Russell 2017; Shabo 2020. For a formulation of the "blind chance" problem earlier in the eighteenth century, see Leibniz's "Fifth Letter" to Clarke (Leibniz and Clarke [1715] 2000, 36–64, esp. §7).

Creuzer, he seems to realize the error of his ways. This would explain why, having exhausted all options up to that point, Kant seems to retreat to his earlier account, defending a form of moral necessitarianism once again in his late *Metaphysics of Morals*.

Before attempting to untangle these problems facing Kant's theory of freedom, some clarification of terms is in order:

Compatibilism	The freedom of an agent's will is compatible with universal determinism, according to which both appearances and things-in-themselves are subject to natural causality.
Incompatibilism	The freedom of an agent's will is incompatible with universal determinism, according to which both appearances and things-in-themselves are subject to natural causality.
Leeway Freedom	The freedom of an agent's will consists of the power to choose from among two or more courses of action.[7]
Source Freedom	The freedom of an agent's will consists in the power to initiate action from itself.[8]
Moral Liberty	The moral law is not the necessary causal law of a free will.
Moral Necessity	The moral law is the necessary causal law of a free will.

If there is a degree of consensus in the literature, it is that the mature Kant rejects all forms of compatibilism in favor of incompatibilism.[9] A further assumption one finds is that by the early 1790s, Kant had modified his theory to include both leeway freedom and moral liberty, thereby conceding the truth of the Objection from Necessity raised by Ulrich. This is why, for example, Kant's rejection of indifference in the *Metaphysics of Morals* has elicited a mixed response from commentators, being either ignored or rejected as

---

[7] Compare this with Crusius's ([1744] 1969, §50) definition of "perfect freedom" (*vollkommene Freyheit*): "Perfect freedom is also called *libertas indifferentiae* or *aequilibrii*. But it does not take place everywhere, but only when two objects are ultimately indifferent [*gleichgültig*] at least according to our insight; or when, under two ends [*Endzwecken*], which we desire in equal degree of strength, we ought to determine ourselves to select one of them"; for discussion, see Walschots 2021. In the more recent philosophical literature, leeway freedom is often treated as equivalent to what Harry Frankfurt (1969, 829) has termed the "principle of alternate possibilities," according to which "a person is morally responsible for what he has done only if he *could have done otherwise*" (emphasis added). Insofar as the principle of alternate possibilities is defined in terms of leeway *power* (or the *ability* to choose indifferently between two or more options), I believe Kant had systematic reasons to reject it.

[8] This is what Kant terms "cosmological," "transcendental," or "absolute" freedom: the power of "an absolute causal spontaneity beginning from itself" (A446/B474).

[9] In Allen Wood's classic 1984 paper "Kant's Compatibilism," Kant is counted as a "compatibilist" in the sense that he argues for the coexistence of freedom and natural necessity. Here I shall take the compatibilist position to refer to its more standard usage as a thesis regarding the *unrestricted* determinism of natural laws. I assume that by the time of his critical period Kant was opposed to this form of compatibilism. For further discussion, see Bojanowski 2012.

inconsistent with Kant's theory of freedom. However, a reexamination of the development of Kant's theory in light of the *Freiheitsstreit* suggests a different story: that from 1781 onward Kant was an incompatibilist who consistently upheld both source freedom and moral necessity. When Kant declared in 1797 that freedom of choice cannot be defined in terms of indifference, he was making explicit a tenet of moral necessitarianism that he upheld for much of his career.[10]

The reading I shall defend in this Element will be controversial on several fronts. First, it challenges a common view about the development of Kant's theory of freedom, according to which he came to embrace the idea of transcendental freedom on the grounds of our ability to do otherwise. On my reading, freedom as absolute spontaneity is not different in kind from the freedom Kant ascribes to a "holy" will: both are instances of lawful freedom oriented to the good (the moral law), the difference being that human freedom is corruptible and hence imperfect.[11] Second, my argument is that Kant never characterizes

---

[10] One finds scholars assuming that Kant's theory of freedom underwent some kind of shift in the *Religion*, considering Kant's explicit distinction between freedom of "will" (*Wille*) and "choice" (*Willkür*). Paul Guyer (2017, 125) defends a strong historical claim that "Kant was always committed to the distinction between *Wille* and *Willkür* even if not in those words, and to the thesis of the freedom of *Willkür* to choose between good and evil, again even if not always in those words." While the view often goes unstated, the claim that Kant was committed to liberty of indifference has been defended by Iain Morrisson (2008) and Marcus Kohl (2015a). (All three views will be discussed in §3.3.) This is by no means a universally accepted reading of Kant, however. Allen Wood (1984, 80) notes that Kant "flatly refuses to define freedom in terms of this indifference [i.e., the capacity to do otherwise]," and further that for Kant "freedom consists in a one-way difference," whereby "freedom consists in the ability to act autonomously even when we do not, but it does not consist in the possibility of acting heteronomously, even if this possibility always does exist for us." Similarly, Halla Kim (2015, 263) speaks of the freedom of *Willkür* as an "asymmetrical freedom without any implication about its ability to do otherwise." Among recent commentators, Colin McClear (2020, 54) also gets it right: "Transcendental freedom in general does not essentially involve *leeway* or the ability to do otherwise. Kant is therefore a *source* rather than a leeway incompatibilist: the key notion of (transcendental) freedom is not the ability to do otherwise, but to be the undetermined causal source of one's actions, insofar as those actions are under one's control." In the very next sentence, however, McClear claims that "for Kant there is nevertheless an important connection between transcendental freedom and leeway, for it is precisely the fact that we can control our actions that makes possible the ability to do otherwise" (55). In my view, this further claim is not warranted, and we shall see in §§2.4–2.5 that Kant does not explain either our control over our actions or our subjection to imperatives with reference to an ability to do otherwise.

[11] The reading I am putting forward bears some resemblance to a line of interpretation defended by Christopher Insole (2013) and Patrick Kain (2021). Their main question is how Kant worked to reconcile human freedom with divine action. Yet they assume Kant's path to the discovery of transcendental freedom was motivated in part by his recognition of an asymmetry between human freedom and divine action: the fact that God always wills the good, but human beings can (and do) fail in such willing. This leads them to conclude that Kant defined transcendental freedom in terms of our "ultimate responsibility" and our "ability to do otherwise" (see Insole 2013, 89; Kain 2021, 316–317). However, the move from lacking

this corruptibility in terms of leeway power, understood as a capacity to choose equally between two or more courses of action. For Kant, immoral action is a fact that must have its source in the agent's will, but his point is that this misuse of freedom is beyond explanation and thus inscrutable. Our awareness of the moral law shows that we are free, and we can understand our faculty of choice as a one-way power to comply with the moral law. But when it comes to the fact of evil, Kant's claim is that we must take responsibility for a deed whose inner mechanism is beyond our grasp.[12]

Here is the plan. After reviewing Kant's reasons for characterizing the moral law as the causal law of a free will (§2.1 and §2.2), I will return to the Free Will Dilemma that Kant's early critics put pressure on (§2.3). I will then defend Kant's theory of freedom from this dilemma by drawing upon two pairs of distinctions: the first between practical necessitation and natural necessitation, the second between noumena and phenomena (§2.4 and §2.5). Lastly, I will trace further developments of the *Freiheitsstreit* in the work of Creuzer, Reinhold, Maimon, and Fichte (§3.1 and §3.2), before criticizing three recent accounts of Kantian leeway freedom (§3.3).

2 Kant's Moral Necessitarianism: Against Indifference

2.1 The Lawless Will: A "Nonentity"

To understand why Kant views freedom as a kind of causality, it is helpful first to consider how he understands the faculty of will as such. This brings us to Section II of the *Groundwork*, where we find Kant defining the will on three separate occasions:

---

determining grounds to the ability to do otherwise receives no further argument. As a result, neither Insole nor Kain considers the possibility I am proposing: that Kant never fully endorsed a liberty of indifference model, even when he came to embrace the idea of transcendental freedom, and that he was consistently committed to moral necessitarianism during the critical period.

[12] Since I am restricting my discussion here to Kant's critical period (from 1781 onward), I shall remain noncommittal with regard to the question of how Kant's theory of freedom evolved during his pre- and semi-critical phases (from the 1750s through to the 1770s). That being said, my view is that the major shift from Kant's early compatibilism to his mature theory of transcendental freedom was not occasioned by a newfound commitment to liberty of indifference, *pace* Hogan (2009a, 2009b). On Kant's mature view, while the will lacks external determination from antecedent grounds in the order of *time*, it does not lack internal determining grounds in the order of *reason*. The latter is what he means by the moral determination of the will through its own law, namely, the principle of autonomy. As I understand it, Kant's solution is not to abandon compatibilism in favor of leeway freedom, as some scholars assume, but to abandon compatibilism in favor of self-legislation. For discussion of the path leading to Kant's first *Critique*, see Insole 2013; de Boer 2020. For an illuminating analysis of Kant's early engagement with Crusius, see Dyck 2016, forthcoming.

Will-1: The will is a capacity to act "according to the representation" (*nach der Vorstellung*) of laws (GMS, AA 4:412).

Will-2: The will is a capacity to "determine itself" (*sich selbst . . . zu bestimmen*) according to the representation of "certain laws" (GMS, AA 4:427).

Will-3: The will is a capacity to determine itself according to the laws of its own "universal legislation" (*allgemein gesetzgebend*) (GMS, AA 4:434).

As we can see, each definition builds upon the former, yielding a more comprehensive view of what it means to will. The first definition, or what I am calling will-1, is the most minimal of the three inasmuch as it says merely that the faculty of will is a capacity to act according to the representation of laws. Will-2 goes further by clarifying the mode of acting in terms of self-determination. Finally, will-3 reveals the kind of laws that are left unstated in the second definition, specifying them in terms of the will's own capacity for universal legislation. A complete analysis of the faculty of will thus yields insight into what Kant calls the supreme principle of morality, namely, the principle of autonomy. As a rule, it states the most general formula of moral action, to the effect that one can, in the maxims one adopts, consider oneself at the same time as giving universal legislation (GMS, AA 4:434). That is the thrust of Kant's argument in Section II: that what morality commands of us is "neither more nor less than just this autonomy" (GMS, AA 4:440).[13]

Given this conclusion, it is not surprising that Kant returns in Section III of the *Groundwork* to the concept of causality. "A *will*," he writes, "is a kind of causality of living beings in so far as they are rational" (GMS, AA 4:446). At first Kant adds that "*freedom* would be that property of such a causality as it can be efficient independently of alien causes *determining* it" (GMS, AA 4:446) – a definition Kant admits is of little value.[14] But he does not stop here, for Kant thinks we can move deeper into the concept of a will and attain a positive grasp of its freedom (as a definition). This brings us to the doctrine of moral necessitarianism, the claim that the moral law is the causal law of a free will. Kant argues as follows:

> [**Premise 1**] The concept of causality carries with it that of laws according to which, by something that we call a cause, something else, namely, the consequence, must be posited. [**Premise 2**] Freedom, though it is not

---

[13] For discussion of the complexities surrounding Kant's notion of autonomy in general, see Ameriks 2000; Khurana 2011; and the contributions in Khurana and Menke 2011.

[14] Cf. KpV, AA 5:55: "In the concept of a will, however, the concept of causality is already contained, and thus in the concept of a pure will there is contained the concept of a causality with freedom, that is, a causality that is not determinable in accordance with laws of nature" (*Im Begriffe eines Willens aber ist der Begriff der kausalität schon enthalten, mithin in dem eines reinen Willens der Begriff einer Kausalität mit Freiheit, d. i. die nicht nach Naturgesetzen bestimmbar*).

a property of the will according to natural laws, is not lawless because of that at all, but must rather be a causality according to immutable laws, but of a special kind; for otherwise a free will would be a nonentity. [**Premise 3**] Natural necessity was a heteronomy of efficient causes; for every effect was possible only according to the law that something else determines the efficient cause to causality. [**Premise 4**] Freedom of the will can only be autonomy, i.e., the property of the will of being a law to itself. [**Premise 5**] The proposition: the will is in all actions a law to itself, designates only the principle of acting on no maxim other than that which can also have itself as its object as a universal law. This is just the principle of morality. [**Conclusion**] Therefore, a free will and a will under moral laws are one and the same. (GMS, AA 4:446–447)

This is a complex passage, to be sure, but for our purposes what matters is premise 2, since it is only by *denying* the possibility of a lawless will that Kant can secure his inference to the claim that a will must have a causal law. The claim that the principle of autonomy is the only suitable candidate for the will's law follows straightforwardly, since all Kant needs to show is that a law exhibiting "heteronomy" (such as a law of natural mechanism) is antithetical to the will's self-determination. For this reason many commentators have found it puzzling that the key premise in Kant's doctrine of moral necessitarianism appears without argument, which to the defender of leeway freedom and moral liberty begs the question. Even if we grant some version of Kant's transcendental idealism and assert that the law of natural mechanism applies only to the world of appearances, why should we think that our noumenal agency is subject to moral necessity? Is it not preferable to think of our phenomenal selves as determined, but our noumenal selves as unconstrained by all rules?

Two initial considerations might speak on behalf of moral libertarianism. The first is that it captures a popular intuition that to be free is to be unconstrained by rules of any kind. In this sense of the term, my freedom consists in my spontaneity, and the more spontaneous I am, the freer I am. We could even say that my freedom is lawless, for there is nothing to stop me from, say, randomly throwing large sums of money into a fire, bursting into song during a lecture, or doing cartwheels down the streets of Toronto. I need not provide reasons for why I did such things, but that does not mean that in doing them I was unfree; indeed, one might think I was freer, since my deeds were unconstrained by any reason. Suppose I had good reason not to throw large sums of money into the fire, but by nevertheless doing so, I proved my freedom – my capacity to rise above all norms of custom or morality or even rationality.[15] On this picture,

---

[15] For discussion of these Dostoevskian themes, see Scanlan 1999.

Kant's claim that a lawless will is a "nonentity" (*Unding*) appears counterintuitive. At the very least, he could have said just that a lawless will is an imprudent will, but instead he made the stronger claim that the concept is self-contradictory.

Another reason we might want to call moral necessitarianism into question is that it creates a potential problem for the imputation of evil to an agent, which itself is a variation of the Objection from Necessity outlined earlier. Reinhold was one of the first readers of Kant to voice this concern, according to which Kant's identification of morality and freedom undermines the imputation of immoral action:

> *Problem of Imputation.* (*i*) If the moral law is the necessary causal law of a free will, then the will is not free when it is not subject to the moral law. (*ii*) An evil will is not subject to the moral law. (*iii*) Therefore, an evil will is not free.

Reinhold did not think Kant was guilty of creating this problem, though he worried that the *Groundwork* and the second *Critique* lend themselves to this misunderstanding. For this reason Reinhold redefines freedom as the ability to act without being constrained either by the laws of reason *or* by the demands of sensibility, adding that someone exhibits free "choice" (*Willkür*) by deciding to "determine himself" by reason or to "let himself be determined" by objects of sensibility (1789, 90). He reiterates this point in the second edition of his *Letters on Kantian Philosophy* (1792), claiming that the will is "the capacity of a person to determine itself to the satisfaction or nonsatisfaction of a desire, either according to the practical law or against it." Reinhold thereby defines freedom as liberty of indifference, or the capacity of choice to act either "for or against the practical law" (1792, 271–272). We are responsible for an evil character, he claims, just as we are responsible for a good character because we are at liberty to choose one or the other.

2.2 The Principle of Determinate Lawfulness

In light of Reinhold's worry, it is natural to ask why Kant ever seemed attracted to moral necessitarianism in the first place. To address this question, we must return to premise 2 of Kant's argument in Section III of the *Groundwork* (quoted earlier) and try to clarify the reasons he had for upholding it. Upon inspection, it is clear that Kant's rejection of the possibility of a lawless will is itself an inference from an unstated principle in premise 1. Recall that premise 2 states that a free will must be a "causality according to immutable laws." Kant later distinguishes between two kinds of laws: those that operate from without (heteronomously) and those that operate from within (autonomously). These remarks follow from what Kant establishes at the beginning of his argument, where he defines the concept of causality in terms of a law that for any cause, a consequence must be posited (see GMS, AA 4:446). What is noteworthy is that Kant has already stated a version of this principle in Section II, that "everything in nature works according to laws" – or what we might call the *Principle of Determinate Lawfulness*:

> *Principle of Determinate Lawfulness*. Everything in nature, whether sensible or supersensible, works according to laws, whether those laws concern what happens (laws of nature) or what ought to happen (laws of freedom).[16]

When Kant formulated this principle earlier in the *Groundwork*, he did so in the context of defining the will: "Only a rational being has the capacity to act according to the representation of laws, i.e. according to principles, or a will" (GMS, AA 4:412). This definition of will-1 and its clarification in what I have termed will-2 and will-3 are crucial steps in Kant's derivation of the supreme principle of morality. But it is only when we arrive at his argument that the moral law is the causal law of a free will in Section III that these earlier definitions come back into play. For Kant's larger aim is to show that, given the Principle of Determinate Lawfulness, nothing happens *without a causal law* – a point he makes clearly in the first *Critique*: that "every effective cause must have a *character*, i.e., a law of its causality, without which it would not be a cause at all" (A538/B566). This is the version of the Principle of Sufficient Reason that Kant held during much of his pre-critical period: that for everything that happens or ought to happen – including "nature" in all its domains – there must be a character or law of its occurrence.

The application of this principle becomes clear when we consider actions or events in the phenomenal world. When we say, "At sea level water boils at 100° C," we are not predicting the outcome based on repeated past experiences of water boiling at this temperature. Rather, the judgment is about an objective synthesis of appearances that operates according to a rule; that is why, barring impurities of water or changes of pressure, water at sea level always boils at 100°C. One event necessarily follows from the other. Moreover, as early as 1755 Kant recognized that for every action or event, all other alternatives are

---

[16] Kant's opposition to phenomenal chance was consistent throughout his career, spanning both the pre-critical and critical periods. In the second *Critique*, for example, he writes: "If then, one wants to attribute freedom to a being whose existence is determined in time, one cannot, so far at least, except this being from the law of natural necessity as to all events in its existence and consequently as to its actions as well; for, that would be tantamount to handing it over to blind chance" (KpV, AA 5:95). Consider also his opening statement in the Preface to the *Groundwork* that the laws of all "determinate objects" belong to one of two classes, "either laws of nature, or of freedom" (GMS, AA 4:387).

excluded. The boiling point of water operates according to a fixed causal rule, which means that all other possible boiling points are excluded from this phenomenon. And this makes sense, given that we would not have a unified experience of the world if water at sea level boiled at 100°C on some days, at 72°C on other days, and at 97°C on still other days. For Kant, the regularity of phenomena is due to the necessity of rules making up our ongoing apprehension of a manifold, which we call the sensible world.

Consider next the application of this principle to the case of a perfectly good agent, or what Kant calls a "holy" will (GMS, AA 4:414). Let us imagine a will unaffected by desires, impulses, or any of the tendencies of self-deception that Kant attributes to the common psychology of human beings. The task is to represent an agent who experiences nothing within herself that could tempt her to question the validity of moral laws. For this special individual, her agency would consist in always acting in accordance with her autonomy: She would always choose maxims that she sees as expressing her standing as a universal lawgiver, while recognizing at the same time that this status puts her on an equal footing with all other members of the moral community. For such an agent, whose will is perfectly good, what she recognizes to be required by the laws of morality would immediately exclude alternate possibilities: a duty to a keep a promise, for example, would strike her as a rule that closes off its violation, including any possible course of action that fails to respect this duty.[17]

My point in introducing this idealized agent is to foreground a symmetry between how the Principle of Determinate Lawfulness applies in the theoretical domain, where we apprehend phenomena in a manifold of experience, and how it applies in the practical domain, where we formulate maxims in a manifold of willing.[18] The character of natural phenomena (such as water boiling at 100°C)

---

[17] As Kant explains: "Thus a perfectly good will would just as much stand under objective laws (of the good), but it could not be represented as thereby *necessitated* to actions that conform with laws, because it can of itself, according to its subjective constitution, be determined only by the representation of the good. Therefore, no imperatives hold for the *divine* will and generally for a *holy* will: here the *ought* is out of place, because *willing* already of itself necessarily agrees with the law" (GMS, AA 4:414). In other words, a holy will's freedom is not diminished by its lack of leeway power or moral liberty; on the contrary, such a lack is the mark of its perfection. As we shall see, a human will displays this structure of choice as a power to act in conformity with the moral law (what Kant in the *Religion* calls its original predisposition to the good). Yet the failure of a human will to orient itself to the good does not presuppose that it has leeway freedom or moral liberty, as I will argue in §2.5. The demands of morality appear to us as imperatives, not because we have the ability to do otherwise, but because of an imperfection of our "subjective constitution," the ground of which Kant considers opaque to us.

[18] See KpV, AA 5:47: "The moral law is, in fact, a law of causality through freedom and hence a law of the possibility of a supersensible nature, *just as* the metaphysical law of events in the sensible world was a law of the causality of sensible nature; and the moral law thus determines that which speculative philosophy had to leave undetermined, namely, the law for a causality the concept of which was only negative in the latter, and thus for the first time provides objective reality to this

is a causal rule that explains why things *happen*; the character of normative phenomena (such as a duty to keep a promise) is a causal rule that explains why things *ought to happen*. In the manifold that we call the sensible world, rules operate to the exclusion of alternate possibilities, and that exclusion is what makes a determinate event of experience possible. Similarly, in the manifold we call the moral world, rules operate to the exclusion of alternate possibilities too, and that exclusion is what makes a determinate act of willing possible. To say that the moral law is the causal law of a free will, then, is to say that the moral law is the rule of the will's self-determination, which as a principle excludes all forms of willing that are subject to external influences.

This helps to bring out the argumentative force of premise 2, if only because it dispels the impression that a will "under moral laws" is somehow *unfree*. Consider again our idealized agent who is conscious of her autonomy and only ever forms maxims that express her recognition of this autonomy. We can imagine her feeling elevated by the awareness that she is a universal legislator subject to no external authority – not even God's – because she is living in accordance with her own faculty of reason. If asked, she would likely say that she feels most free whenever she acts under moral laws, because she sees herself at the same time as a legislator of those laws. Considered from this standpoint, the rest of humanity – all of us who pursue our desires at the expense of our duties – appear to be so many "slaves of passion" who are less (not more) free for acting randomly or doing whatever we wish. For the idealized agent, the exclusion of alternate possibilities demanded by the moral law is not a negative restriction: rather, it is a condition of her will's perfection, that of being an independent, spontaneous, and self-legislating power.

Kant's further point is that what makes the will of a finite rational being different from natural phenomena like boiling water is that the will is a causal power that admits of degrees of perfection. The conformity of the will to its inner law – the moral law – is a special kind of normative restriction that corresponds to the will's elevation because it is self-imposed. Thus, the person who feels more free the more she acts in accordance with the laws of morality is not deceived, in Kant's view. For she correctly feels that her self-imposed restriction under moral laws is a perfection of her will as a causal power, one that in principle excludes influences – even those stemming from her sensibility – that undermine her autonomy. In this sense, acting according to moral laws does exclude alternate possibilities, and to that extent it limits rather than expands one's leeway liberty, but not in a way that decreases one's freedom.

---

concept" (emphasis added). For a different account of this symmetry, with which I broadly agree, see Watkins 2019, chap. 11.

If we represent to ourselves the upper limit of the will's perfection, as in the case of a holy will, we can see that there is no freedom to do otherwise because such a will excludes nonmoral courses of action, and yet its freedom is still absolute. Thus the Principle of Determinate Lawfulness is the unstated basis for Premise 1, which led Kant to say that a lawless will is an absurdity. The will, like everything in nature, must have a law of its causality or character, "without which it would not be a cause at all." That law cannot be a principle of natural causality because such causality operates from without, conflicting with the will's self-determination. The only law left is the principle that the will is a law to itself, which is the moral law *qua* principle of autonomy. Hence, the character of a free will is that of acting on maxims it can also recognize as universally legislating. And that is why the will is a causal capacity to initiate action "from itself" (*von selbst*): its restriction to the moral law is at the same time an expansion and elevation of its power. The more a finite rational being approximates the ideal of such power – the ideal of "holiness" – the more it excludes actions that are contrary to morality. As Kant explains, there is no power to do otherwise built into the definition of freedom; acting contrary to the law is not a *Vermögen* (an *ability* or *power*) but an *Unvermögen* (MS, AA 6:227).[19]

Another way to unpack this line of argument is to think of lawfulness in terms of unity.[20] For Kant, every power of the mind has a supreme principle, a governing law of its use, and he is clear that this law is what makes each power both unifying and unified. Sensibility is a power of receiving a manifold of empirical intuitions, and its supreme principle is to bring those intuitions under the unity of space and time. Understanding is a power of combining such a manifold, and its supreme principle is to bring it under the "unity of apperception" (B136). Reason is a power too, and for Kant its legitimate use is to direct all faculties toward "architectonic unity," whereby all parts of human cognition are "purposively united with each other as members of a whole in a system of

---

[19] Compare with Refl 3868: "The *Vermögen* for actively willing the known good that is in our power is freedom; but the faculty for willing the known evil the hindrance of which is in our power does not belong equally necessarily to freedom. The latter is not really a *Vermögen*, but a possibility of being acted upon. Evil actions certainly stand under freedom, but do not happen through it." See also Refl 3856, dated to around 1764–1768: "In the case of freedom, to be determined means not to be passive, either through the way in which objects affect or through a highest productive cause. I can say: at this moment I am free (*liber aut devinctus*) and unconstrained to do what I prefer; yet it is unavoidably necessary that I act thus. It is a law of self-activity, which makes the opposite impossible. Even with regard to the morally evil, one can be determined by just such a free resolve. No! One can be determined to that only passively or not at all, because the free will always remains and thus cannot be constrained at all, but does not always exercise its activity."

[20] This is a theme of Christine Korsgaard's (2009) more recent work that I think has not been fully appreciated. See also Stephen Engstrom's (2009) sophisticated reconstruction of Kant's philosophy along similar lines.

human cognition" (A835/B863; cf. A298/B355). For Kant, on my reading, the power of willing is no different: the more we perfect the power, the more we bring our maxims under the unity of moral laws.

2.3 Noumenal Determinism and Ulrich's Fork

Nevertheless, the initial worries behind the *Freiheitsstreit* still remain with us. As mentioned in §1, the point that Ulrich wanted to make in his *Eleutheriology* (1788) is that, rather than protecting freedom from the forces of necessity, Kant has only reintroduced those forces by making the will subject to the moral law's causality at the noumenal level. Kant is committed to making natural necessity rule without exception over the world of appearances, he explains, including the empirical character of our will. Yet the empirical character of our will is, by Kant's lights, grounded in an intelligible character whose causality must operate according to laws as well. According to Ulrich, we have "necessity with the immutability of the intelligible character (albeit not natural necessity in the Kantian sense)," the result being that "necessity reigns here too" (1788, 32). Nor does Ulrich believe that Kant avoids the problem by redefining freedom as the power to choose otherwise, that is, liberty of indifference, since that would raise a problem of "indeterminism." Because a power to choose otherwise is a power without "decisive reasons," the will is thereby reduced to mere "chance" (1788, 21).

At the heart of Ulrich's criticism is the claim that between necessity and chance there is no third alternative. This we might call *Ulrich's Fork*:

> *Ulrich's Fork.* There is absolutely no middle way between necessity and chance.[21]

Looking back, we can see how this fork might be a problem for Kant's Principle of Determinate Lawfulness. Recall that our discussion in §2.2 was meant to show why being restricted to a rule does not necessarily limit a power. Restriction to a rule of natural causality is what makes my cognition of actions or events in a sensible manifold determinate, and the application of that rule to specific phenomena is what allows for a unified experience of the world. Working toward systematic unity of cognition under the rule of reason is also a progressive perfection of my mind. However, restriction to that rule does not limit my mind: conformity to the law of any cognitive faculty is what gives that faculty *unity*, and its progressive perfection, for Kant, is what enhances its *power* – it does not diminish it. And yet, to play devil's advocate on Ulrich's

---

[21] This is the title of section 6 of Ulrich's *Eleutherology*: "Es gibt schlechterdings keinen Mittelweg zwischen Nothwendigkeit und Zufall" (Ulrich 1788, 21).

behalf, we might point to an asymmetry between the theoretical and practical domains. This is because, however active the mind is in its cognitive operations, only a pure will exhibits what Kant calls "absolute spontaneity," and it is here that symmetry between the two domains no longer holds.

As it turns out, Kant does not need perfect symmetry between the theoretical and practical domains to make his argument work. In various texts he is explicit about the fact that spontaneity of sensibility and spontaneity of understanding are both relative, since they both display a degree of dependence on a given manifold of intuition (see A546/B574; GMS, AA 4:452). Reason is a unique power in this regard, since its operations are elevated above sensible intuition; and the "cosmological" freedom of reason in its pure practical use – the pure will – is the most elevated of all, since it is a causal power to initiate action *von selbst*, as Kant says (A446/B474). My point in drawing parallels between these applications of reason is only to show that everything that happens or ought to happen stands under a causal rule, as its character or law.[22] While some might find it attractive to argue from the spontaneity of theoretical cognition to freedom of will, this is not an option for Kant, especially since he believes that it is only consciousness of the moral law that "discloses" our freedom to us (see KrV, AA 5:29–30).[23] The relevant point here is that only the connection between moral law and will is the right kind of causal connection for autonomy; all else counts as "heteronomy."

Turning the tables now on Ulrich, we can say that the Objection from Necessity rests on an equivocation between two distinct senses of "causal connection." For simplicity, let us call an *autonomous* causal connection "*a*-causal" and its corollary necessity "*a*-necessity," and call a *heteronomous* causal connection "*h*-causal" and its corollary necessity "*h*-necessity." With these distinctions in place, the premises of the Objection from Necessity are more precise:

(1) (MORAL NECESSITARIANISM) The moral law is the necessary *a*-causal law of a free will.

---

[22] There has been some debate recently about how to understand the modal status of Kant's theory of freedom, with several commentators framing the freedom-nature divide in terms of the "contingency" of choice and the "necessity" of natural laws (see, e.g., Watkins 2004, chap. 5). Uygar Abaci (2022) gives compelling reasons for questioning this interpretive setup, and I find myself sympathetic to his "non-modalized" account of noumenal freedom; for a different reading, see Stang 2016. It goes without saying that all talk of modality at the noumenal level is "merely heuristic and regulative," as Kant says, and we have no grounds to attribute necessity or contingency to things-in-themselves (see A617/B645). Thanks to Eric Watkins and Allen Wood for pressing me to clarify this point.

[23] For an extended defense of this interpretation, see Ware 2014, 2017, 2021. For an important discussion of why freedom is only an object of subjectively necessary belief/faith (*Glaube*), see Willaschek 2017.

(2) A will subject to the *h*-causality of the moral law is determined.

(3) (NOUMENAL DETERMINISM) Therefore, a moral will's activity reduces to *h*-necessity.

The slide in meaning from premise 1 to premise 2 makes all the difference. For once we assume that the will is subject to a heteronomous causal law (*h*-causality), it follows that the will's activity reduces to heteronomous necessity (*h*-necessity), leaving us with the problem of noumenal determinism. However, the original version of the Objection from Necessity begs the question to the defender of *a*-causality and *a*-necessity. Nothing about the argument demonstrates that such causality/necessity is impossible; instead, it assumes that all causality/necessity must be of a heteronomous (or mechanistic) variety.[24]

To avoid the objection, all we need to do is write the premises consistently:

(1) (MORAL NECESSITARIANISM) The moral law is the necessary *a*-causal law of a free will.

(2*) A will subject to the *a*-causality of the moral law is determined.

(3*) (NO NOUMENAL DETERMINISM) Therefore, a moral will's activity reduces to *a*-necessity.

Now this raises the question: What are *a*-causality and *a*-necessity? Everything turns on this, since Ulrich's Fork – the claim that there is "no middle way between necessity and chance" – is a problem for Kant's theory of freedom only if by "necessity" he means *h*-necessity exclusively. To preempt the Fork, all we need to do is establish grounds for distinguishing *autonomous* causal connections from heteronomous ones. If we can do this, securing premise 2*, we can show that the *a*-causality and *a*-necessity of a moral will enhance the will's freedom, securing conclusion 3*. This would yield an important payoff – that Kant's moral necessitarianism does not entail noumenal determinism after all.

2.4 Necessitation and Causality

While Kant has left many resources to secure premise 2*, the most relevant concerns a pair of distinctions he often draws in his critical work: (a) the distinction between practical necessitation and natural necessitation, and (b) the distinction between noumena and phenomena.[25]

---

[24] This calls to mind a thesis maintained by many scholastic thinkers, according to which freedom is compatible with a certain kind of necessity ("necessity of immutability") but not compatible with external determination ("necessity of coercion"). For discussion, see Hoffmann 2019.

[25] For an instructive overview of these distinctions and their relevance for understanding Kant's reply to the Objection from Chance, see Dunn 2015.

To begin with, we can understand necessitation as such in line with the claim that everything in nature operates according to laws – what I have termed the Principle of Determinate Lawfulness. Necessitation will then refer to the way laws govern things, namely, by excluding alternate possibilities and applying to all cases of a kind. Necessitation is "natural," according to Kant, (*i*) when the causal connection lies between two appearances *qua* phenomena, and (*ii*) when the causal connection lies between two appearances in time. The time condition is already contained in the first definition, but it serves to bring out the following rule of natural necessitation:

> *Natural Necessitation.* For any given action or event E, there must be a cause C, and that C must be antecedent in the order of time, at t_1, such that the determination of E at t_2 excludes all possible non-E's.

This highlights a distinctive feature of natural causality and its form of necessitation. In terms of time relations, all effects are preceded by an infinite series of antecedent conditions, since for every cause of an effect (as the rule states) there must be a prior cause, which in turn must have a prior cause, and so on *ad infinitum*. As Kant puts it in the first *Critique*, the unrestricted version of the law of natural causality rules out the possibility of cosmological or transcendental freedom, the power of beginning a new series "from itself," since all causal connections in nature must be preceded by antecedent states in time. This is why Kant adds that for the "physiocrat" – the person who believes that "all is nature" in this narrow sense of the term – freedom is a nonentity, an "illusion of the mind" (A449/B477).

Before turning to this objection, let us consider what the concept of nonnatural necessitation contains. We now know that necessitation as such refers only to the way laws govern things (by excluding alternate possibilities and applying to all cases of its kind). If natural necessitation occurs (*i*) when the causal connection lies between two appearances (*qua* phenomena), and (*ii*) when the causal connection lies between two appearances in time, what might *nonnatural necessitation* look like? As a matter of definition, it must be a necessitation that does not lie between phenomenal appearances in time. So what might that be? Kant's answer is that practical necessitation is still a species of causality, but one that operates through concepts, where the representation of concepts provides an agent with *ends* she ought to realize *through her willing*.[26] Thus the

---

[26] See A547/B575: "Now this 'ought' expresses a possible action, the ground of which is nothing other than a mere concept, whereas the ground of a merely natural action must always be an appearance." Compare with the *Prolegomena* (AA 4: 344–345): "We have in us a faculty that not only stands in connection with its subjectively determining grounds, which are the natural causes of its actions – and thus far is the faculty of a being which itself belongs to appearances – but that

structure of practical necessitation is similar to that of natural necessitation, since it operates through a twin process of determination and exclusion of alternatives:

> *Practical Necessitation.* For any given maxim M, there must be a cause C, and that C must be antecedent in the order of reason such that the determination of M excludes all possible non-M's.[27]

This distinction lies behind what Kant says in the first *Critique* about the two ways we can think of causality in general. "In respect of what happens," he writes, "one can think of causality in only two ways: either according to nature or from freedom," to which he adds:

> The first is the connection of a state with a preceding one in the world of sense upon which that state follows according to a rule. By freedom in the cosmological sense, on the contrary, I understand the faculty of beginning a state from itself, the causality of which does not in turn stand under another cause determining it in time in accordance with the law of nature. (A533/B561)

Kant's further point is that nonnatural causality is conceivable only at the level of things-in-themselves, since all relations between appearances trigger an infinite regress that forecloses any causal power beginning from itself. That is why the rule of Practical Necessitation makes no reference to time determinations. For any given maxim M, there must be a cause C, and that C must be antecedent in the order of reason, and for Kant this must be an *intelligible* order rather than a temporal one. His example of getting up from a chair is helpful to consider here: for when I get up from a chair, I initiate an "absolutely new series, even though as far as time is concerned this occurrence is only the continuation of a previous series" (A450/B478). From the standpoint of appearances, the event of getting up is tied to a chain of causes extending back in time infinitely. From an intelligible standpoint, by contrast, my act does not lie "within the succession of merely natural effects and is not a mere continuation of them," but counts rather as an "absolutely first beginning of a series of appearances"

---

also is related to objective grounds that are mere ideas, insofar as these ideas can determine this faculty, a connection that is expressed by *ought*. This faculty is called *reason*."

[27] In the case of moral necessitation, the exclusion of alternate possibilities refers to any action contrary to the principle of the will's autonomy. This does not rule out the possibility of moral error, understood as an imperfection of willing that consists of making exceptions to the demands of morality. As we shall see in §2.5, the misuse of freedom in making exceptions can still coexist with the moral law's causal operation. This is important for my reading, as I want to lay emphasis on the *endless perfectibility* of the power of choice (*Willkür*) to harmonize with its own legislative will (*Wille*). See Appendix A for further discussion.

(A450/B478; cf. A553/B581). Yet this makes sense only if we distinguish between these two domains, the phenomenal and the noumenal.[28] This helps to clarify the nature of the autonomous causality (or *a*-causality) that underpins the doctrine of moral necessitarianism. As a matter of definition, *a*-causality cannot be a causality that operates at the level of appearances, since that would reduce to heteronomy, with each event being preceded by antecedent events in time. More positively stated, and still as a matter of definition, *a*-causality must operate at the intelligible level of concepts, which leaves open the possibility of transcendental freedom, the power to initiate a new series from itself. The reason why *a*-causality can have only one law is because there is only one law consistent with the will's independence from external influences. As we know, the supreme principle of morality just is the principle of autonomy, which states as a rule that the will can always recognize in its maxims its own giving of universal legislation. There is only one principle consistent with the idea of a self-generating causal power, and that is the moral law.[29]

Remember too that for Ulrich's Fork to pose a real problem, it must be true that there is an exclusive disjunction between heteronomous necessity on the one hand and chance on the other. But there is no such disjunction, since it is conceivable to represent a form of necessity that results from nonnatural (and so nonheteronomous) causality: this is the necessity of a will acting according to the principle of its own universal legislation, whereby its activity is from itself and so fully spontaneous. *Pace* Ulrich, the claim that the moral law is the causal law of a free will does not entail noumenal determinism, since the causality in question is consistent with the will's independence. This allows us to say, having established premise 2*, that a will subject to the *a*-causality of the moral law is "determined" (3*), without the determination in question undermining its freedom; rather, this is the kind of self-determination that marks the

---

[28] One might still wonder whether transcendental idealism raises potential problems for Kant's practical philosophy. Two such issues, considered by Joe Saunders (2016, 2017), is that it becomes difficult to account for the possibility of intersubjective recognition and for degrees of responsibility. I flag these concerns here without further comment, but it is worth noting that versions of these two worries were already voiced by Kant's early successors, especially the problem of recognition.

[29] This answers a question left open by commentators such as Karl Ameriks (2003) and Clinton Tolley (2006), who interpret the status of moral laws in Kant's system as essential (and in that sense "real") principles of a pure will, rejecting the more common "constructivist" reading of such laws as chosen or taken up by us. The mystery, however, is how we can make sense of the fact of moral error if not by invoking the libertarian thesis that moral laws are binding on us (as what we "ought" to do) because we can always act or will otherwise. While this issue goes beyond the scope of this Element, I believe that interpreting Kant as a metaethical "realist" about the source of moral laws coheres better with the account of freedom I am defending, since it explains the way in which only moral willing manifests a genuine "power" of free choice. Because the principles of morality constitute the *essential capacity* of freedom, there is no leeway for adopting normative principles at one's discretion.

perfection of the will, not its destruction. A will that restricts itself to the same principle it gives to itself is not less free, but more free.[30] The idea of an intelligible ground then allows us to use the category of causality in new ways. From a theoretical standpoint, this category applies only to the sensible domain of cognition; Kant's point, however, is that this same category acquires new significance in connection with the intelligible domain of volition. And this is worth emphasizing, as it explains the contrast between the concept of causality according to nature and that of "causality from freedom."[31] Since the order of priority that makes up the space of an intelligible ground can refer only to an order of reason and not to an order of time, the causality of the moral law can refer only to a normative relationship between a "ground," the idea of a self-legislating *Wille*, and its "consequence" for our power of *Willkür*, namely, to act in accordance with the law.[32] Any cause-effect relation that pertains to the phenomenal world is mechanistic – and so antithetical to freedom – since it mandates that for every action or event in time there must be a prior action or event. For Kant, the space opened up by transcendental idealism allows us to *redeploy* this category to show how a power of absolute spontaneity beginning from itself can still count as a lawful power.

Having reached this conclusion, it is worth pausing to reflect on where we stand in the dialectic of the *Freiheitsstreit*. As we have seen, the controversy developed into the form of the Free Will Dilemma, forcing Kant to define freedom of will in a way that reduces it either to necessity (the first horn) or to blind chance (the second horn). Ulrich was the first critic who argued that Kant is guilty of reintroducing the problem of determinism at the noumenal level by defining the moral law as the causal law of a free will. I have attempted to preempt this criticism by showing that it turns on an equivocation between two senses of causal necessity; for once we keep this distinction in view, the

---

[30] See V-Met/Dohna, AA 28:678: "To be able to compel oneself is the highest degree of freedom – to be able to necessitate oneself through one's own reason." Compare again with Anselm ([1080–1086] 2007, chap. 1): "A will that cannot fall away from the rectitude of not sinning is freer than a will that can abandon that rectitude" (*Liberior igitur est uoluntas quae a rectitudine non peccandi declinare nequit, quam quae illam potest deserere*).

[31] By far Kant's most sustained defense of this point is in the second *Critique*: see KpV, AA 5:6, 15, 16, 32, 44, 46, 47, 48, 49, 50, 54, 55, 65, 69, 78, 89, 95, 98, 103, 104. See also MS, AA 6:221: "In reason's practical use the concept of freedom proves its reality by practical principles, which are laws of a causality of pure reason for determining choice independently of any empirical conditions (of sensibility generally)."

[32] Kant often prefers to speak of the order of reasons in terms of "imperatives." Categorical imperatives "determine the conditions of the causality of a rational being as an efficient cause," he writes, "only with the respect to the will, whether or not it is sufficient for the effect" (KpV, AA 5:20). In his example, a law against lying promises counts as a categorical imperative because the question is only whether the law, as a ground, is sufficient to determine the power of choice accordingly, as a necessary effect. Thanks to Ryan Wines for pressing me to clarify this point.

Objection from Necessity loses its force. But then even if this is true, what are we to make of the second horn of the dilemma? And what can we say about Kant's apparent acceptance of a liberty of indifference view in his 1792 essay "On the Radical Evil of Human Nature"? Is this one place where Kant leaves himself exposed to the Objection from Chance?

In §2.5 I will argue that it does not. Kant understands that the Objection from Chance is a problem for theories of leeway freedom and moral liberty, I believe, and that is why he is consistently committed to source freedom and moral necessity.

2.5 Responsibility for Evil

There are few places in Kant's published or unpublished work where he defines freedom of will as the ability to do otherwise, as the ability to choose for or against the moral law, or any similar formulation. This is not because philosophers of his day lacked the terminology to describe this position: The phrase *libertas indifferentiae* was in wide circulation well before the eighteenth century, and it was central to the work of Kant's older contemporary, Christian August Crusius (1715–1775). In one of Kant's first publications, the *New Elucidation* of 1755, we even find a mock dialogue between a defender of determinate grounds (Kant's position at the time) and a defender of leeway freedom (the position of Crusius and his followers), and it is instructive to see how he frames the thesis of leeway freedom:

> Personally, I should think that if you eliminate everything which is in the nature of a connected series of reciprocally determining grounds occurring in a fixed order, and if you admit that in any free action whatever a person finds himself in a state of indifference relative to both alternatives, and if that person, even though all the grounds which you have imagined as determining the will in a particular direction have been posited, is nonetheless able to choose one thing over another no matter what – if all that is conceded, then I should finally admit that the act has been freely performed. (PND, AA 1:402)

In reply, Kant's interlocutor accuses this proponent of leeway freedom of ruling out any explanation of why the agent acts one way rather than the other, thereby reducing the will's activity to a "product of chance" (PND, AA 1:402). Curiously, this line of criticism reappears in Creuzer's *Skeptical Observations on the Freedom of the Will* (1793). By defining freedom as the capacity to choose for or against the moral law, Creuzer upholds, we must think of the will as subject to two ruling forces, at one time reason, at another time sensibility, without having any determining ground to explain what compels the agent to choose one over the other (128 n).[33] If Kant did read Creuzer's book, he would have had a feeling of *déjà vu*, for this was the same objection he had raised against Crusius thirty-five years earlier. Now, in a strange turn of events, it was being leveled against Kant himself.

The issue here is not merely interpretive, however. Even if we evade the Objection from Chance by showing on textual grounds that Kant was never committed to leeway freedom, we must still address a conceptual worry surrounding his doctrine of moral necessitarianism (what I have termed the Problem of Imputation). To recall, Reinhold was concerned that defining the moral law as the causal law of a free will would render immoral action unfree, which would make it impossible for us to impute evil to a rational being: an unfree agent can be no more responsible for evil than a natural disaster is. This does not fit with Kant's repeated insistence that human beings are responsible for both their moral and immoral deeds. On Reinhold's view (as we saw in §2.1), the only solution is to characterize freedom as the power to choose for or against the moral law. But if Kant never adopted that view, as I am claiming, then what could he say in response to the Problem of Imputation?

As a preliminary step, it is important to see that Reinhold's account rests on the following assumption:

> *No Indifference, No Imputation.* If the will does not have liberty of indifference to act for or against the moral law, then it cannot be held responsible for acting one way rather than the other.

Reinhold himself never argued directly for this claim, perhaps because he thought it was self-evident that leeway freedom is the only kind of freedom that can support moral imputation. Yet we have reason to question this, quite apart from how we interpret Kant, since it raises anew the specter of chance. If there is no determinate ground for my willing one way rather than the other, then it seems that my willing is a product of blind chance. Moreover, it is no help to the libertarian's case to raise this exercise of will to the noumenal level, since noumenal chance would be just as problematic as chance at the phenomenal level. I say this only to emphasize that the Problem of Imputation on its own does not mandate a commitment to leeway freedom or moral liberty. If moral libertarianism threatens to undermine the concept of freedom, then it faces an even worse version of the imputation problem, since it potentially renders *both* moral and immoral action mysterious.[34]

---

[33] In this context Creuzer cites letter 15 from Friedrich Jacobi's 1785 book on Spinoza, according to which a capacity that is completely lacking in determining grounds amounts to a "non-entity."
[34] This problem was first noted by Maimon; see §3.1.

Arguably, the doctrine of moral necessitarianism faces a less daunting challenge, for it has only to explain how immoral action counts as *free* action. I believe Kant left enough hints to show why a commitment to source freedom and moral necessity does not rule this out a priori. The first point to note is that Kant never equates (1) resistance to acting according to the moral law with (2) a genuine *Vermögen* (power or ability). Nor, relatedly, does he ever say that finite rational beings can have an incentive to do evil for the sake of evil, or – which amounts to the same thing – that they can have a reason to violate the moral law for the sake of violating the moral law. Kant makes these points with such frequency that their import can sometimes be lost; but they are key aspects of his moral necessitarianism. To say that the moral law is the causal law of a free will means that it is the supreme norm for the will's unity. It is supreme, for Kant, because it is the only law consistent with the idea of autonomy, the only principle according to which I can regard myself at the same time as a universal lawgiver.

Putting these claims together, it becomes clear why Kant says that a "diabolical" agent is a contradictory concept (RGV, AA 6:35).[35] A diabolical agent, if such an agent were possible, would be someone who freely acts against the moral law, not because of a random whim or inclination, but because he has an incentive for such a violation; in short, he is someone who wills evil for the sake of evil. But this means that he is someone whose exercise of free will operates against his own free will: the very condition of his choice of maxims, the supreme norm of their unity, is not made the object of self-deception or exception-making (as Kant believes is the case for ordinary human evil[36]). Rather, we are to imagine an agent for whom acting against the condition of his own acting is itself somehow a reason for acting. Inasmuch as this is a contradiction of concepts, a diabolical will is not possible. And this supplies further evidence for Kant's commitment to the thesis that the moral law never stops operating as a "causal law" for finite rational beings, since it never loses its place of *authority* as the will's highest determining ground.

But then the question becomes: Are not those self-exceptions that make up the scope of human evil freely chosen? And are they not chosen with at least some degree of awareness of the moral law's authority? If so, it would appear that even those more mundane forms of human evil are performed contrary to the moral law, and hence are "unfree" by the lights of moral necessitarianism.

---

[35] Cf. Refl 3867, composed around 1764–1771: "No one counts as freedom the faculty of being able to desire what is worthy of being abhorred (evil)." For helpful discussion of Kant's argument against diabolical evil in the *Religion*, see Tenenbaum 2007.

[36] Whether this explains weakness of will is another issue, which I set aside here. For further discussion, see Tizzard 2021. For an excellent account of the phenomenon of "rationalizing" in Kant's moral psychology, see Sticker 2021.

In reply, I think this conclusion is too quick, since it does not recognize the fact that a causal law of a power can coexist with a *misuse* of that power. All the doctrine of moral necessitarianism states is that the moral law is the necessary *a*-causal law of a free will. This means that a power to initiate a new series from one's will is possible only under the rule of one's autonomy; thus the moral law is the only principle that makes the will a transcendental power and cosmological ability. However, the doctrine does not rule out the internal diminishing of this power through weakness, or its corruption through impurity, or even a perversion of it through self-conceit. All the grades of the "propensity to evil" we find listed in the *Religion* are so many ways of misusing freedom, but none of them amounts to a power or ability.[37]

On the contrary, these grades of the propensity to evil – weakness, impurity, self-conceit – are so many grades in the imperfection of the will, and for Kant an imperfection always disempowers a faculty, never the reverse.[38] Nor do these grades of imperfection unseat the moral law from its place of authority in the mind of a rational agent, for Kant believed that human immorality always occurs as a form of self-deception or exception-making. We never pursue evil for the sake of evil, but we do try to work our way around the moral law, by questioning its strictness, its purity, or its validity. Because the moral law is the causal law of a free will, we cannot renounce it without, *per impossibile*, renouncing our freedom. These cases of moral failure, considered as so many degrees of imperfection, are not instances of a *Vermögen* at all. Given that they do occur, Kant is committed to saying that they are possible (since actuality

---

[37] This part of my account seeks to build upon the suggestive, albeit brief, remarks that Allen Wood (1984, 81) makes about the possibility-power distinction: "Not every possibility is a power. Some possibilities, in fact, are due to a lack of power." For a superb account of theoretical error in Kant's philosophy, see Engstrom 2009, esp. chap. IV, §4; in relation to our capacity to judge, Engstrom explains, the source of error cannot lie in the capacity itself (since that capacity is only ever guided by a judgment's validity as knowledge), but rather must lie "in the *misuse* of the capacity" (110). My argument here is that the same can be said about our power of choice. Engstrom too distinguishes between the power of judgment (which always accords with the form of knowledge) and the possibility of error (which strictly speaking is not a power or capacity at all).

[38] This point might be lost on readers of the Cambridge translation of the *Religion*, which renders *Willkür* as "power of choice." When Kant speaks of a "choice" in the adoption of an evil character, he is not referring to the concept of an ability or power (*Vermögen*). Even a passage that may be an exception to this rule (RGV, AA 6:31) where Kant writes "Also kann ein Hang zum Bösen nur dem moralischen Vermögen der Willkühr ankleben" can be read as a general claim about the location of the propensity to evil (in freedom). In this context, it is noteworthy that in his preparatory notes for the Preface and Introduction to the *Metaphysics of Morals*, Kant argues that *Willkür* is "free to do or leave undone what the law commands," adding that *Wille* is "free in a different manner" because it is "*legislative* and does not obey the law of nature or any other law, and in this way freedom is a positive capacity [*Vermögen*], not to choose something, since there is no choice here, but rather to determine [*zu bestimmen*] the subject in relation to the sensible [element of] action" (VAMS, AA 24:249).

entails possibility)[39] – but at no point does he characterize the choice of an evil character as a real ability, nor does he define freedom in terms of an ability to do otherwise.[40]

One reason why Kant's readers have at times thought he was committed to moral libertarianism is that his appeal to the actuality of human evil always comes with the admonition that "we *ought* nevertheless to be good." Such an "ought" claim seems to imply that in those situations where we have given in to weakness, impurity, or self-conceit, we *could* have done otherwise, on the grounds that "ought implies can." But this conclusion, however self-evident it might appear, rests on a false inference. It is correct to say that when we ought to have acted according to the moral law we could have done so; but this does not entail that at the moment when we failed to act according to the moral law, we enjoyed that place of which the moral libertarians speak: the place where we stand indifferently between two or more courses of action. For Kant, there is no such place – it is an *Unding*. We are not in fact indifferent to the moral law; its commands resound "unabated in our soul," as Kant says (RGV, AA 6: 45), and those commands do not go away when we fail to exercise our power of freedom. Even in those instances of moral failure that we call evil, Kant claims, the moral law remains within us.[41]

---

[39] I agree with Timothy Aylsworth that if freedom is incomprehensible – and we have good textual grounds for attributing this view to Kant – then we should "avoid asking any questions whatsoever about how conversion is possible" (2020, 285). On my view, this thesis requires the supplementary principle just introduced, that actuality implies possibility, since that principle secures the right inference from the fact of evil to its possible ground in an agent's will. For further discussion, see Kemp and Iacovetti 2020.

[40] I think this is consistent with Allison's reading, although there is room for interpretation here. In his 1990 book, *Kant's Theory of Freedom*, Allison concludes that "Kant's claim, then, which is certainly a reasonable one, is that only a being with freedom, positively construed as the capacity for self-determination on the basis of rational grounds (the capacity to act according to the conception of law), can be meaningfully conceived to have a *corresponding capacity* to deviate from the dictates of reason" (1990, 136, emphasis added). In his 2020 book, *Kant's Concept of Freedom*, however, Allison drops this language of "capacity" altogether, writing now that the choice of evil "is not the result of a capacity but of a failure to exercise one that we possess" (2020, 266). As he explains, the key to the coherency of Kant's position lies in a distinction (drawn in Refl 3868) between actions "standing under freedom" and actions "happening through" freedom. Any instance of evil belongs to the former category, as evil is imputable to an agent (and in that sense "stands under freedom"), whereas only those actions proceeding from duty express a genuine ability or power (and in that sense "happen through" freedom). So far as things stand, I agree with Allison's 2020 assessment; however, I worry that Allison may be creating an unnecessary burden for his account by attempting to fill in the mystery of evil, which he characterizes in terms of "the all-too human propensity to incorporate into one's maxims inclinations or desires which reflect the interests of the subject and would lead to courses of action that knowingly violate the moral law" (2020, 466). My proposal is that all Kant needs to do, once he has secured the agent's ultimate responsibility for evil by positing its source in the agent's freedom, is to invoke a thesis of incomprehensibility and let matters rest. For a well-argued account of Kant's commitment to the inscrutability of evil, see Tenenbaum 2021.

[41] Compare this with Kant's "hardened scoundrel" in *Groundwork* III, who is "conscious of a good will that, by his own acknowledgment, constitutes the law for his evil will as a member of the

In my view, this is not a departure from Kant's account in the *Religion*; rather, it sheds light on what he was trying to defend throughout much of his career. As he says in the *Metaphysics of Morals*:

> We can indeed see that, although experience shows that a human being as a sensible being is able to choose in opposition to as well as in conformity with the law, his freedom as an intelligible being cannot be defined by this, since appearances cannot make any supersensible object (such as free choice) understandable. (MS, AA 6:227)

One might think that this conflicts with Kant's argument in the *Religion* that for evil to be imputed to an agent, it must be ascribed to his freedom of choice at the noumenal level – specifically, in his adoption of an evil "disposition." On my reading, there is no tension here, for in the *Religion* Kant only ever argues from the empirical fact that human beings can and do act immorally, to the condition of the possibility of acting immorally. His point is that because this condition cannot emerge from a natural series of time determinations – for then it would not be free – we must ascribe it to a human being's intelligible character,[42] which is not subject to such time determinations.[43]

---

world of sense – a law of whose authority he is cognizant *even while he transgresses it*" (GMS, AA 4:455, emphasis added).

[42] One might wonder how this bears upon Kant's so-called Incorporation Thesis, his claim that "freedom of choice [*Willkür*] has the characteristic, entirely peculiar to it, that it cannot be determined to action through any incentive *except so far as the human being has incorporated it into his maxim* (has made it into a universal rule for himself, according to which he wills to conduct himself); only in this way can an incentive, whatever it may be, coexist with the absolute spontaneity of the power of choice (of freedom)" (RGV, AA 6:23–24). While a full analysis of this thesis falls outside the scope of this Element, I wish to voice my agreement with Richard McCarty (2008), who argues that this requirement bears primarily upon the selection of one's "disposition" (*Gesinnung*). This is a key qualification – and a departure from the standard reading of incorporation as pertaining to individual maxims – since it suggests that Kant was *positing* the spontaneity of choice (at the noumenal level) as a basis for *imputing responsibility* for the adoption of one's moral character. The appearance of leeway freedom in the phenomenal realm, whereby we seem to display an ability to do otherwise, must have its source in freedom (via an act of "incorporation"). But notice that Kant is not tempted to define this noumenal "deed" in terms of a multidirectional power of indifference. Indeed, the remainder of the passage suggests a different picture: "Now, if the law fails nevertheless to determine somebody's free power of choice with respect to an action relating to it, an incentive opposed to it must have influence on the power of choice of the human being in question; and since, by hypothesis, this can only happen because this human being incorporates the incentive (and consequently also the deviation from the moral law) into his maxim (in which case he is an evil human being), it follows that his disposition as regards the moral law is never indifferent (never neither good nor bad)" (RGV, AA 6:24).

[43] These considerations show why the anthropological interpretation of evil advanced by Allen Wood (1999) is basically correct. On Wood's reading, Kant is following in the footsteps of Jean-Jacques Rousseau (1712–1788) in characterizing evil as a kind of inflamed self-conceit (or *amour-propre*) rooted in comparative self-evaluations. Wood argues further that the conditions of self-conceit are social in character, stemming from systems of oppression that make up an unequal society. The rejoinder that critics of this interpretation often make is that it locates evil in the empirical world, and this contradicts Kant's claim that evil arises from one's noumenal will

In drawing this inference, all Kant is saying is that the evil we witness in the world must have its source in our freedom. He is not making the further inference that scholars sometimes draw on his behalf: that we have a genuine power to choose for or against the moral law at the noumenal level. For Kant, ascribing liberty of indifference to an agent's will would commit the fallacy of defining a thing-in-itself through a thing-as-it-appears. Certainly, experience provides examples of such indifference, but the question is only whether we have grounds to define freedom in such terms. On my reading, this is what Kant wants to avoid. "For it is one thing," he writes, "to accept a proposition (on the basis of experience) and another thing to make it the expository principle (of the concept of free choice) and the universal feature for distinguishing it" (MS, AA 6:227). In the *Religion*, when Kant ascribes evil to an agent's intelligible character, he is careful to speak of it as a corruption of an agent's original predisposition to the good, adding that it is a "mystery" we cannot comprehend.[44] To say that evil is the result of an ability to do otherwise would be, by Kant's lights, to overstep the bounds of what we can know.[45]

When Kant refers to *evil*, moreover, he is careful to gloss "corruption" (*Verderbtheit*) with the Latin *corruptio* (RGV, AA 6:30); in this way he places his discussion within a broadly Augustinian framework for thinking about evil

---

(see Grenberg 2009; for an attempt to find a middle ground, see Russell 2020). However, once we view evil as a corruption of free choice (in the quasi-Augustinian sense of the term), we can see that while the propensity to evil must be located in one's noumenal will, its conditions of activation can only appear to us *under empirical conditions*. Kant himself is clear that the inclinations on their own are innocent, but that the empirical conditions that give rise to the corruption of freedom reflect the society in which we live. This is why Kant devotes so much of the *Religion* to explaining why the "restoration" of human beings to the good is possible only as a social project, one that works to eliminate inequality.

[44] As Kant puts it later in the *Religion* (AA 6:43): "There is no conceivable ground for us, therefore, from which moral evil could first have come in us." It is difficult to imagine how Kant could have stated this claim more emphatically. For an admirable discussion of Kant's "incomprehensibility thesis," see Aylsworth 2020.

[45] Though it was not in the context of the problem of evil, Kant had already sketched an answer along these lines in the first *Critique*. "Reason," he writes, "does not belong at all in the series of sensible conditions which make appearances necessary in accordance with natural laws. It, reason, is present to all the actions of human beings in all conditions of time, and is one and the same, but it is not itself in time, and never enters into any new state in which it previously was not; in regard to a new state, reason is determining but not determinable" (A553/B581). This is why, Kant adds, "one cannot ask: Why has reason not determined itself otherwise? But only: Why has it not determined appearances otherwise through its causality? But no answer to this is possible. For another intelligible character would have given another empirical one" (A553/B581). Elsewhere Kant is clear about the fact that the image of a conflict between good and evil within the human will is only an allegorical representation "on analogy of two independent principles dwelling in the human being" (Prog, AA 20:347). Thus his account in the *Religion* in no way purports to define noumenal freedom as an indifferent power between a good and an evil character.

as a *deprivatio, negatio,* or *defectus.*[46] Though we cannot conclude from Kant's choice of terms here that he is alluding specifically to Augustine,[47] it does give us a clue for understanding how a misuse of our ability of choice is a corruption of it. The idea of evil as a corruption of choice speaks to why Kant rejects liberty of indifference, since a *corruptio* is strictly speaking the removal or destruction of something; thus, to corrupt one's power of choice by choosing evil is to be deprived of that power. So when Kant said that the ground of evil cannot be located in the "*corruption* of the morally legislative reason," his point is that the causality of freedom cannot "uncause" itself. That would be "as if reason could extirpate within itself the dignity of the law itself," which Kant argues is "absolutely impossible." To regard oneself "as a freely acting being, yet as exempted from the one law commensurate to such a being (the moral law), would amount to the thought of a cause operating without any law at all, . . . and that is a contradiction" (RGV, AA 6:35).[48]

3 The Reception of Kant's Theory of Freedom

3.1 The Controversy Continues

In the spring of 1793, Kant received the following letter:

> Most distinguished and honorable man!
> Herr Professor! Great and worthy sir! Please receive the heartfelt thanks of a young man, to whom your admired writings have given so much important instruction, so much illumination and reassurance on the dark path of this earthly life. – How many veils have fallen from my eyes since I first read your work, and all-blissful faith has never left my heart, contrary to what the false apostles say: "You would be afraid of the light!" – Yes, honourable teacher! If ever a philosophy were able to bring the head and heart of human beings into harmonious unison, then it would be yours. I am

---

[46] Cf. V-Mo/Mron II, AA 29:615, where Kant speaks of "departure from the moral law" in terms of "culpable depravity of action," using the Latin *pravitas actionis peccatum.*

[47] Regardless of direct influence, it is not difficult to trace the kind of moral necessitarianism upheld by Kant to a constellation of scholastic theories inspired by Augustine, according to whom the essence of freedom does not consist in a leeway power to do otherwise. For the classical formulation of this thesis, see *De civitate Dei* 5.10 (cf. *De perfectione iustitiae hominis* 4.9 where Augustine speaks of the "happy necessity" grounding "true freedom"). One can imagine Kant agreeing with Augustine's letter 127 (often cited by Aquinas) that "Fortunate is the necessity which compels to what is better!" (cited in Hoffmann 2019, 201; see also Hoffmann 2019 for discussion). Another relevant background source is Anselm's *De libertate arbitrii* (*On Freedom of Choice*), especially his definition of free choice as the "power [*potestas*] to preserve rectitude of will for the sake of rectitude itself" ([1080–1086] 2007, chap. 3). Thanks to Martin Pickavé for directing me to this text. For discussion of Kant's debt to the Stoic tradition, see Sensen 2011 and Merritt 2021.

[48] Considering that Kant's argument here repeats the doctrine of moral necessitarianism from *Groundwork* III, it is puzzling that this passage has not drawn more attention from scholars who think Kant turned to a liberty of indifference theory in the *Religion.*

so deeply convinced of this truth that I expect from it, with the calmest resignation, the most reassuring explanation of the final doctrine, the doctrine of the freedom of will. It must please you to give this teaching yourself – to clear away all the difficulties that have oppressed previous theories of freedom, as you have begun to do in the April 1792 issue of the *Berlinische Monatsschrift*. If I may be so bold as to contribute to this end, I attach here a little book as a small token of my sincere admiration and heartfelt gratitude. I would consider myself immeasurably rewarded for my labor if you, most venerable sir, wanted to take some consideration of it. (letter 568, AA 11:422–423)

This letter is dated April 7, 1793, and its author was none other than Leonhard Creuzer, then twenty-five years old, who had just published his "little book," *Skeptical Observations on the Freedom of the Will*. We can surmise from the fact that Kant received this letter that he was aware of the *Freiheitsstreit* his theory had set in motion. However, there is no evidence that Kant replied to Creuzer, or that he ever read his book.[49] We can only speculate what Kant would have thought about the Objection from Chance that Creuzer wanted to raise against theories espousing liberty of indifference. As it happens, some-one close to Kant's philosophy took on the task of writing a review of Creuzer's study for the *Allgemeine Literatur-Zeitung*, which appeared in the October 1793 issue. The review was left unsigned, but the reading public would soon learn more about its author, Johann Gottlieb Fichte (1762–1814), to whom we shall return below.

Kant's awareness of the *Freiheitsstreit* is also evinced in a letter he received from Salomon Maimon (1753–1800) on November 30, 1792 (letter 548, AA 11:389–393).[50] The letter was composed soon after Reinhold published

---

[49] One can imagine that if Kant did read it, he would have been happy to see Reinhold's indifferentism taken to task, but he would not have appreciated his position being lumped together with Reinhold's. Creuzer took issue with Kant's claim in his 1792 essay that the ground of one's character must itself be a "deed of freedom [*Actus der Freiheit*] (for otherwise the use or abuse of the human being's choice [*Willkür*] with respect to the moral law could not be imputed to him, nor could the good or evil in him be called moral)" (RGV, AA 6:21). Quoting this passage, Creuzer argues that Kant's essay contradicts his commitment to lawful freedom, citing as evidence Kant's claim from *Groundwork* III that freedom, "though it is not a property of the will according to natural laws, is not lawless, but must rather be a causality according to immutable laws" (Creuzer 1793, 149). Creuzer understands Kant's supposedly new view to consist in a form of lawless choice at the noumenal level, that is, the level at which one adopts the subjective ground of one's maxims (whether good or evil). In Creuzer's estimation, this saves Kant's theory from the horn of determinism, only to get it caught – "just like Reinhold" – in the horn of indifferentism, reducing his concept of freedom to a "nonentity" (147).

[50] "Even now that I have read the second part of his [i.e., Reinhold's] *Letters*, I notice that his concept of free will leads to the most inexplicable indeterminism. You posit freedom of the will in the hypothesized causality of reason. According to him, on the other hand, the causality of reason in itself is a natural necessity. Reinhold therefore explains free will as 'a faculty of the person to determine himself, with regard to the satisfaction or non-satisfaction of the selfish

the second edition of his *Letters on Kantian Philosophy*, which included a new discussion of the free will problem in the eighth letter, entitled "Exposition of the Concept of the Freedom of the Will." Surprised by Reinhold's commitment to moral libertarianism, Maimon wrote to Kant that Reinhold's concept of a free will "leads to the most inexplicable indeterminism" (AA 11: 390). As he explains, Kant's theory of freedom involves a "causality of reason," and yet on Reinhold's alternative "the causality of reason would be a natural necessity" (AA 11: 390). Further, he argues that on Reinhold's view of freedom as the capacity to do otherwise, either for or against the moral law, the resulting definition does not "in the least" concern itself with the "determining ground" of freedom (AA 11: 390). In other words, Maimon was voicing a version of the worry Kant had long felt regarding the notion of liberty of indifference: that it runs afoul of the Principle of Determinate Lawfulness. Maimon perceived this as well from the standpoint of his commitment to the Principle of Sufficient Reason, and he was keen to know what Kant thought of Reinhold bringing his theory under the banner of indeterminism.[51]

Maimon went on to pose this question in a series of letters he wrote to Reinhold himself, later published in a collection titled *Quarrels in the Field of Philosophy* (1793), asking how the will can decide between two opposed drives and what reason it can give for selecting one over the other. "The question," he states, is why the will "in one moment follows the instruction of reason, and in another moment the selfish drive" (233). Maimon confesses that he cannot understand this, and this leads him to formulate a version of the Free Will Dilemma according to which the Reinholdian will reduces to either natural necessity or blind chance:

First horn   If the two opposed drives are opposed as "effective forces," where the stronger one wins and determines the action of the will, then the will is not free but depends on "natural laws." (233–234)

Second horn If the will is not determined by the stronger of the two drives, then its actual decision (either for the selfish drive or for the unselfish drive) depends on blind "chance" (*Zufall*). (234)

As this makes clear, the source of the dilemma is Reinhold's brand of leeway freedom, his claim that the will can choose between the operations of reason and

---

drive, in accordance with or contrary to the demand of the unselfish' – without in the least worrying about the determining reason" (letter 548; see AA 11:389–393).

[51] I here leave aside the details of Reinhold's theory of indifferent choice; suffice it to say that Reinhold wanted to uphold a notion of indifferent choice without succumbing to the Objection from Chance. For more detailed discussion, see Walsh 2020; for a sympathetic but ultimately critical reading of Reinhold's efforts, see Noller 2018.

sensibility. For Maimon, as soon as we accept such indeterminism about the will, there is no way to explain how the will can determine itself to act at all. The concept of an indifferent will is thus an "empty" concept, since by violating the Principle of Determinate Lawfulness, it amounts to what Maimon called a "powerless power," which is simply a figment of thought.

Reinhold for his part did not receive these criticisms gratefully:

> I let the will depend on chance!! Have you read the seventh and eighth letters! I let the will depend on itself – it is not chance, but a first cause, an absolute cause in relation to its effect. Can you not think of an absolute cause? I can. . . . Every cause thought merely through reason is absolute, and every absolute cause is free, because the ground of its effect is contained only in itself. . . . These are for me matters of fact. Are they not also for Herr Maimon? (Maimon 1793, 235–236)

That Reinhold frames his question in these terms is revealing. For it shows that by characterizing freedom as a causality "from itself" – alluding to Kant's definition at A446/B474 – Reinhold thinks he has protected his theory from the Free Will Dilemma. When pressed by Maimon about the determination of choice for or against the moral law, he reverts to this definition. Therein lies his problem, however, for Kant's point is that there is only one way to think of freedom as a power beginning from itself, and that is in terms of the moral law. Answering Reinhold's question, Maimon sallies back: "Can I not think of such a capacity? Oh yes! It is precisely how I think of nothing [*Nichts*]," to which he adds: "*Nothing* has no ground. *Nothing* has no results. It is not actual, not possible, etc." (1793, 240). But Maimon does not need to press these further claims. All he needs to say is that liberty of indifference amounts to "nothing" – a concept without reality – because as soon as we formulate the law of free causality we end up with Kant's doctrine: moral necessitarianism.

3.2 Giving the Law, Being Determined

This is not an option that Maimon himself pursued, nor does it appear in the review of Creuzer's book that Fichte published in the *Allgemeine Literatur-Zeitung* (Fichte [1793] 1846). Instead, Fichte appears to take Reinhold's side by exonerating him of the charge of noumenal determinism. As Fichte initially frames the issue, Creuzer's objection is that the definition of freedom agreed upon by Reinhold and Kant – according to which one has the "capacity [*Vermögen*] to determine oneself in absolute self-activity to obey or disobey the moral law, and hence to act in diametrically opposing ways" – violates the "law of logical ground"

(Fichte's label for the Principle of Determinate Lawfulness) (412). Fichte's response is that "Reinhold has thoroughly refuted this possible objection in advance," referring to his 1792 *Letters on Kantian Philosophy*. And yet Fichte qualifies his praise in the next sentence: "It is this reviewer's conviction, which he affirms with full respect for this great and original thinker, that Reinhold has neither indicated nor overcome the basis of the misunderstanding in question" (412–413). In the rest of his review, Fichte adds a few (highly compressed) observations of his own.

As we read Fichte's review further, it becomes clear that his deference to Reinhold is, much like Creuzer's deference to Kant, somewhat artificial. This is not evident at first, since Fichte's initial point is that we must be careful to distinguish between (1) the "act of *determining*, as a free action of the intelligible I" and (2) the "*determinate being*, as an appearing state of the empirical I" (413). The former is what he means by "self-activity," his preferred term for "will" (*Wille*), and the latter is what he means by "choice" (*Willkür*) in its empirical character. The will is originally "formless," Fichte writes, because it is what gives the moral law; it is only the restriction of the will to this principle that appears in consciousness as a "fact" of being bound to that law. For this reason, Fichte argues, the will *qua* self-activity never appears in consciousness, but is merely a "postulate" we must assume as the ground of our determinate acts of choice: "The will never appears as determining, but always as determined" (413). All of this is consistent with Reinhold's account.

On the basis of this distinction, however, Fichte then asks whether self-activity of the will is the cause of what we feel in experience as a capacity to do otherwise, where we appear to be at liberty to determine ourselves in the direction of reason or sensibility:

> If one answers this question affirmatively, as Reinhold actually does (see p. 284 of the Eighth Letter, where he says "the freedom (of the will) is fully comprehensible to me from its *effects*, by means of which it occurs among the *facts of consciousness*," etc.), then one draws something intelligible down into the series of *natural causes*, and is thereby also misled into displacing it into the series of natural effects; that is, one is misled into assuming something intelligible that is not intelligible. (414)

Fichte in turn wants to separate the self-activity of the will as a determining power from the appearance of this determination as choice; for his claim is that the appearance of a capacity to act for or against the law pertains only to the latter. The point is simple enough, yet it carries important implications. What Fichte finds Reinhold guilty of doing is taking a property of choice in its empirical expression for a property of the will in itself. In saying this, he anticipates a claim Kant makes four years later in his *Metaphysics of Morals*:

> Although experience shows that a human being as a sensible being is able to choose in opposition to as well as in conformity with the law, his freedom as an intelligible being cannot be *defined* by this, since appearances cannot make any supersensible object (such as free choice) understandable. (MS, AA 6:227, emphasis added)

Anticipating Kant's point, Fichte adds that the "source of this misunderstanding can be eliminated only by returning to what seems to this reviewer to be the true spirit of the Critical philosophy" (414). For Fichte, this requires going beyond the terms of the *Freiheitsstreit* itself.

Up until 1793, this controversy had revolved around the dilemma of reducing the will's activity to necessity or chance, and all the main players of the controversy had defined their positions in response to this problem, as was the case with Ulrich, Schmid, Reinhold, Creuzer, and Maimon. In Fichte's view, this dilemma is averted once we distinguish between the free causality of the will (as *Wille*) and its determinate appearance in a natural series (as *Willkür*). Why? Because worries about noumenal determinism and noumenal chance go away, Fichte maintains, once we define freedom as a form of self-activity that does not proceed from a chain of antecedent causes. The will is what gives the moral law to itself, and through this inner restriction to the norm of its own causality it thereby determines itself. Once this determination occurs, willing manifests in a lawful form, and this is when the *appearance* of a capacity to act otherwise appears on the scene. The problem Fichte thinks needs a solution, then, is how *Wille* and *Willkür* can agree – how an original act of self-determination can harmonize with its empirical character.

The solution Fichte goes on to propose, in the "spirit" of Kant's philosophy, rests on a novel version of the doctrine of pre-established harmony:

> According to the law of natural causality, a real ground in a previous appearance must be assumed for the appearance of a determined being. But the being-determined by the causality of nature (*Willkür* as phenom-enon) and the being-determined by freedom (*Wille* as noumenon) must agree. The ground of this agreement can lie neither in nature, which has no causality over freedom, nor in freedom, which has no causality in nature, but only in a higher law, which includes and unites both. That higher law can only be, as it were, a predetermined harmony. Therefore, it is neces-sary to assume a kind of predetermined harmony that unifies a free causality and its determination in a natural series. (414–415)[52]

---

[52] For further discussion, see Martin 2018.

As to *why* we must assume such harmony in the first place – the central assumption of the argument here – Fichte offers no direct support, although he does leave the reader with a hint by writing that one must assume such harmony for the sake of a "moral world order" (*moralischen Weltordnung*; 414). Fichte also suggests that this need for a higher law unifying freedom and nature is "Kant's true opinion," and that Kant is committed to demonstrating "that freedom must have a causality in the world of the senses" (415). Among the places in his writings where such a higher law appears, the most compelling, on Fichte's view, is Kant's appeal in the *Religion* to a "higher assistance" coming to aid a human being's moral regeneration to the good. Concluding the review, he adds that this doctrine of higher assistance is "so intimately woven" into the spirit of Kant's philosophy that it is "laughable" that Creuzer failed to understand it (a shortcoming we may forgive Creuzer now, as this same doctrine has puzzled Kant's readers ever since).

When Fichte wrote this review, he had yet to discover the principle that would allow him to do what Kant perhaps thought was impossible, namely, to demonstrate a causality of freedom in nature according to a higher legislation (what Fichte would later call the principle of the "pure I"). Nevertheless, this early review is valuable for showing us how the *Freiheitsstreit* was beginning a fresh turn in the year 1793. While Fichte finds Reinhold guilty of defining an intelligible faculty ("freedom of will") according to its empirical appearance ("liberty of indifference"), he seems to agree with Creuzer that liberty of indifference is not a power attributable to transcendental freedom as such. We also find evidence that Fichte sides to some extent with Kant's moral necessitarianism, as when he remarks that the pure will can determine itself in only one way, under the moral law. Still, the argument of his review shows signs of moving in a different direction, as Fichte does not think that the dilemma between determinism and indeterminism captures the central problem of freedom. As he states, the central problem is how the determinate appearance of choice in a natural series can harmonize with its freely legislated ground; and Fichte believes that only a doctrine of predetermined harmony can remove the appearance of this tension.

One cannot help but think that in saying this Fichte was sidestepping the Free Will Dilemma instead of resolving it. The problem of how my actions in a natural series of time determinations can agree with the spontaneity of my will is akin to what Kant had set up in the first *Critique* as the antinomy between freedom and mechanism. As we have just seen, Fichte's proposal is that showing how a causality of freedom in nature is possible requires a doctrine of predetermined harmony, such that freedom and nature unite under a higher legislation (the principle of the "pure I"[53]). But even if we grant that Kant's system needs such a higher principle, the question to put back to Fichte is how freedom of will is compatible with immoral choices, and this brings us back to the Problem of Imputation. For if my freedom of will is causally governed by the moral law, then the question of how my violations of that law count as free choices remains a puzzle even within a system of predetermined harmony. Nothing Fichte says in his review of Creuzer sheds light on this.

3.3 Kantian Indifference: Three Recent Accounts

Turning now to the contemporary literature, some two hundred years after the *Freiheitsstreit*, it is curious to find a number of scholars defending a version of Reinhold's theory of indifference – with or without reference to Reinhold – on the grounds that it is the only way to explain how immoral action can still count as free action.

Paul Guyer (2017), for instance, has argued that Kant is committed to liberty of indifference, one that defines freedom as the "ability to choose between alternatives," adding that a non-liberty theory is "impossible to reconcile with Kant's account of imputation in the *Religion*" (124 n). He builds his case on Kant's distinction between *Wille* and *Willkür* along with the principle that ought implies can. Guyer suggests that it is not difficult to consider *Wille* to be the source of the moral law's unconditional bindingness, and that what it discloses to the agent is its freedom of *Willkür*, understood as a multidirectional power to form maxims either in conformity with the law or against it. "What the moral law discloses to us," he writes, "is just that we always can choose to act in accordance with the moral law – that we have the capacity to choose for it, even though we also have the *capacity to choose against it*" (137, emphasis added). The point of Kant's distinction in the *Religion*, Guyer maintains, is to make this more precise by showing that one's power of choice is always "free to choose to make the moral law its fundamental maxim or not, and imputable for choice either way" (123–124).

In drawing this conclusion, Guyer expresses agreement with a similar account put forward by Iain Morrisson (2008), who claims that "Kant's concept of practical freedom grounds the notion that one could always do otherwise (i.e. freedom of indifference)" (90). On Morrisson's reading,

Kant's commitment to indifference follows from his notion of "practical freedom," or the capacity to be independent from "pathological necessitation" (Kant's phrase for the motivational force of one's sensible nature). "To claim that we are necessitated by our sensibility," Morrisson writes, "is just to deny that we have the ability to do other than that which our sensibility demands. To deny necessitation (as Kant's notion of practical freedom does) is, therefore, to allow for a capacity to do otherwise" (90–91). For textual evidence, Morrisson highlights a point Kant reportedly made during lecture, to the effect that it is not possible to conceive of pathological necessitation in a human being because freedom consists in this, "that he can be without compulsion in the pathological sense; nor should he be compelled in that way. Even if a man is so constrained, he can nevertheless act otherwise" (V-Mo/Mron II, AA 29:617). For Morrisson, this is evidence that Kant viewed freedom in terms of a leeway power.

Lastly, Marcus Kohl (2015a) has worked to reconstruct Kant's commitment to indifference along the lines of Kant's distinction between perfect, or "holy" wills and imperfect, or "human" wills. What is demanded by the moral law, Kohl explains, presents holy wills with no set of alternate possibilities, because they are immediately moved to do the right thing. For human wills who are afflicted by countervailing interests and inclinations, there is no direct connection between (1) recognition of duty and (2) motivation to act from duty. As Kohl observes, "an imperfect will's recognition of the right reasons cannot inevitably lead to right action because such a will faces alternatives or obstacles to right action"; hence, "when an imperfectly rational deliberator recognizes the force of normative reasons, any rational influence would leave her with the option to go against those reasons" (335). Indifference of choice – for or against the law – is a feature of our imperfect rational agency, a reflection of the fact that our recognition of duty does not come with sufficient determining grounds to form our maxims in accordance with the law.

By way of reply, let us begin by reexamining the text cited by Morrisson, which is admittedly one of the few places where Kant appears to align his theory of freedom with liberty of indifference.[54] In the full passage from the student

---

[54] In what some scholars consider an unreliable source – the *Lectures on the Philosophical Doctrine of Religion* (1783–1784) – Kant is reported to have said that "if the human being is to be a free creature and responsible for the development and cultivation of his abilities and predispositions, then it must also be within his power to follow or shun the laws of morality" (AA 28:1113).

notes based on Kant's 1785 lectures on ethics, he is reported to have said the following:

> Can I really conceive of a pathological compulsion in a human being as well? Truly I cannot, for freedom consists in this, that he can be without compulsion in the pathological sense; nor should he be compelled in that way. Even if a man is so constrained, he can nevertheless act otherwise. Hence it is improperly called compulsion when we are necessitated by such impulses to do a thing, or leave it undone. The moral compulsion can be resisted. The more a man considers a moral act to be irresistible, and the more he is compelled to it by duty, the freer he is. For in that case he is employing the power he has, to rule over his strong inclinations. So freedom is all the more displayed the greater the moral compulsion. (V-Mo/Mron II, AA 29:617)

In isolation, the passage cited by Morrisson gives the impression that Kant entertained the idea that to be free is to enjoy the multidirectional power to act otherwise. A different picture begins to surface when we read it in its full context. All Kant is saying in this lecture is what he repeated time and again in his published work: that the human faculty of choice enjoys practical spontaneity, which he defines in terms of independence from pathological compulsion. The faculty of *Willkür* is always free in this sense of the term because human agents, unlike animal agents, are not compelled necessarily to act on their impulses and inclinations. Notice too that Kant's passing remark about acting otherwise appears in this context, that is, when a human being is said to be constrained to act on the promptings of his sensible nature. Kant's point is that even when such promptings appear overwhelming, our choice remains independent. To say that such an agent "can nevertheless act otherwise" is only to specify this negative characteristic of spontaneity (i.e., lack of pathological necessitation), not a further power of indifference.[55]

The rest of the passage quoted above is instructive, as we find Kant drawing a link between moral compulsion and freedom along the lines considered earlier. Because freedom of will is causally governed by the moral law, conformity of choice to the inner law of freedom admits of degrees. The more one's choice aligns with the moral law (in forming maxims out of a recognition of oneself as their universal legislator) the more one is autonomous. This follows from Kant's denial of liberty of indifference, since spontaneity of choice can realize its independence from

---

[55] In Refl 4226, composed around 1764–1770, Kant expresses this point well: "Freedom does not consist in the fact that we might have preferred the opposite, but only in the fact that our preference was not necessitated." Cf. KU, AA 5:210.

sensibility by forming maxims that accord with the moral law. The more one's *Willkür* harmonizes with the law of its own *Wille*, the more that faculty of choice is free – and Kant even adopts a special term for the perfection of *Willkür*, calling it "autocracy" (MS, AA 6:383). When we actualize a resolved commitment to morality, we bring the empirical character of choice closer to its original idea, the predisposition to the good making up each person's noumenal self. The result is a genuine power over sensibility (autocracy) that aligns with the will's essence of being a law to itself (autonomy) (see MS, AA 6:383).

This speaks indirectly to Guyer's point about the moral law disclosing one's capacity to choose freely "for or against" the law (2017, 137).[56] As Guyer maintains, Kant believes that freedom would not be an item of consciousness were it not for a command to act in ways which (in principle) run contrary to one's inclinations. The question to ask, however, is whether Kant intends to characterize the freedom we encounter via our awareness of the moral law in terms of a leeway power, and that I find less certain. Speaking generally, it would be odd for Kant to say that the moral law reveals, the moment we become conscious of it, our multidirectional power to act for or against this law. This would make for a mixed moral message, saying "You ought always to form your maxims in accordance with this principle," but with the added proviso, "And you enjoy leeway freedom."[57] One might think that the uncon-ditional bindingness of the moral law is meant to close off possibilities that run counter to its principle rather than opening them up. So it is not obvious to me how a power of indifference, or an equilibrium between options, could emerge from such a law itself.[58]

A more specific point to consider is that even if the moral law does not entail leeway freedom, it also does not preclude moral error. I gather that what motivated Reinhold's theory of indifference – and what continues to make this position attractive among some Kantians today – is that if we lose

---

[56] I discuss this particular Kantian doctrine at greater length in Ware 2021.

[57] As I am framing this issue, the worry is that leeway freedom is not consistent with the *form* of the moral law itself – namely, its form as an *unconditional* command that applies categorically and rules out *all* exceptions. Even in the *Groundwork*, we learn that an unconditional command, or practical law, "does not leave the will at liberty to do the opposite [*dem Willen kein Belieben in Ansehung des Gegentheils frei läßt*], so that it alone brings with it that necessity which we require of a law" (GMS, AA 4:420).

[58] If there is a kernel of truth in the idea of leeway freedom, it is that unlike holy agents, we are not necessarily motivated to act in conformity with the moral law. Anthropological evidence shows that moral evil is a fact, and moral philosophy requires us to posit the ground of this fact in our noumenal character, yet the inner dynamics of evil remain beyond the reach of our understanding.

a capacity to do otherwise, immoral actions can no longer be imputed to us.[59] Nonetheless, we have good reasons to think that Kant is able to secure responsibility for evil without adopting leeway freedom. His guiding principle is that actuality entails possibility, and the empirical fact that evil exists in the world suffices to show that it must have been freely chosen, since otherwise it would not be moral evil at all. To make Kant's position more precise, we can say that the one-way power of choice to live up to the principle of its own will excludes a genuine *ability to act otherwise*, but it does not exclude – and this is the key point – the *possibility of corruption*. My morally legislated will can demand that I ought to **A**, and directing my choice to **A** is the only exercise of my spontaneity that brings me closer to autocracy. I then lack the ability to stand indifferently between **A** and **not-A**, but this does not make **not-A** an impossible course of action.[60]

None of this entails that Kant is committed merely to the logical possibility of moral imperfection. As Kohl (2015a) rightly points out, this would run the risk of trivializing Kant's theory of evil. I agree with Kohl, on both interpretive and systematic grounds, that Kant is committed to representing evil as a real opposition to the moral law rooted in an inner "deed" (the propensity to reverse the order of incentives and place self-love above the moral law). However, I do not agree that this commits Kant to anything like a liberty of indifference view; in fact, I think it requires the opposite. Indifference implies an equilibrium between opposing forces, a zero point between **not-A** and **A**, whereas resistance

---

[59] Another common view one finds in the literature is the following (often unstated) argument: (1) Moral "ought" claims are binding upon us only because we can fail to comply with them; (2) failure to comply with moral "ought" claims presupposes leeway freedom or our ability to do otherwise; therefore, (3) moral "ought" claims presuppose our ability to do otherwise. With the argument thus formulated, however, it is clear that its conclusion is not Kant's position, nor does the argument hold together. The key to the argument is premise 2, that failure to comply with moral "ought" claims presupposes our ability to do otherwise. But this premise is unwarranted, since our failure to comply with such claims can be an expression of a corruption or defect of our power of choice and so not a genuine ability after all. With respect to Kant's principle that "ought implies can" (OIC), it is also important to observe, as Uygar Abaci (2022) does, that Kant's version of OIC states only that when we act immorally we have the capacity to act morally; it does not also state the converse, that when we act morally we have the capacity to act immorally. Only the "*moral* ought" implies a power of choice to act from duty, and there is no "ought *not*" that implies we have a power to act from self-conceit.

[60] For a clear reconstruction of this argument, see Korsgaard 1996. With certain qualifications, I am sympathetic to what Korsgaard calls the "Argument from Spontaneity," according to which the will is not on "equal footing" between (1) a choice to make the moral law the condition of following self-love (yielding a "good" character) and (2) the choice to make self-love the condition of following the moral law (yielding an "evil" character) (166–167). Korsgaard has clarified (in personal correspondence, October 2022) that "the argument from spontaneity doesn't rule out the possibility of evil. But it isn't something we freely choose; or rather, it's more like a form of unfreedom that we freely choose, as if we jumped away from our own freedom. That's why it's inexplicable."

implies a countervailing force, an active **not-A** to any given **A**. That Kant characterizes evil in terms of active resistance is a reason to reject rather than affirm leeway freedom, since the latter would occupy a strange place – what Kant calls the zero point between a positive and negative force – and it is not clear how well that sits within Kant's general metaphysics of forces.[61] At any rate, we have seen in §2.5 that active resistance does not require a "power," technically speaking, all the more so given Kant's frequent suggestions that evil is a misuse of freedom.

Nevertheless, Kohl offers the important insight that acting contrary to the moral law must always be an "option" for imperfect rational agents like ourselves (2015a, 353). I agree, so long as we distinguish an "ability" from an "option," and specify the latter as a corruption rather than a power. To say that the moral law is the causal law of *Wille* does not rule out the possibility of *Willkür*'s imperfection and error; that was Reinhold's mistaken inference. Moral imperfection is always a possibility for us because unlike the kind of holy agent described earlier, we are afflicted with tendencies to weakness, impurity, and self-conceit, and these tendencies create a real tension between how we in fact structure our choices and how we ought to be. For Kant, we enjoy no liberty of indifference and no equilibrium between opposing powers. We are always in the battle, as it were, struggling between a devil on one shoulder and an angel on the other. The devil is who we become when we put ourselves above the law; the angel is our true self, who is both the law's master and servant. In the end, Kant understands moral life as an infinite task: the closer we approach the law of autonomy, the greater our freedom.

4 Concluding Remarks

The passage from the lectures on ethics cited by Morrisson (2008) does suggest that Kant was attracted to the idea of leeway freedom. Considered within the broader context of the lecture, however, I have argued that Kant's remarks were not meant to imply that we have an ability to choose for or

---

[61] In the transcripts taken by Mrongovius during Kant's metaphysics lectures in 1782–1783, we find a topic devoted to "Indifference and Equilibrium," which begins with a strong denial of freedom of indifference. Kant is reported to have considered the idea that a human being is free when, faced with two or more options, he indifferently – and hence without determining grounds – chooses one over the other. "But no," the notes read, "he will rather do neither of them" (V-Met/Mron, AA 29:901), a point we find a few sentences later: "A human being in a complete equilibrium will not be able to choose anything" (AA 29:901). In the background of this discussion is the well-known Buridan's Ass argument, according to which an ass with equal amounts of thirst and hunger will die if placed midway between a pail of water and a stack of hay. Versions of this scenario were often used to argue against equilibrium theories of indifference.

against the law. Rather, they cohere with what we have learned in this Element – that Kant was committed to source freedom, and that he defined perfection of choice in terms of degrees of freedom that bring one closer to the inner law of one's own will, the moral law. As for evidence showing that Kant was opposed to liberty of indifference, we have had occasion to consider his comments in the *Metaphysics of Morals*, where his rejection of such liberty is hard to deny.[62]

Still, some readers may feel inclined to think that Kant entertained this kind of model earlier in the 1790s, perhaps under the pressure of the critiques made by Ulrich, Schmid, and Reinhold, and that he changed his mind again only later on. For these readers it will be helpful to consider a passage from the *Religion* itself where Kant's denial of indifference is unmistakable:

> There is no difficulty in reconciling the concept of freedom with the idea of God as a *necessary* being, for freedom does not consist in the contingency of an action (in its not being determined through any ground at all), i.e., not in indeterminism ([the thesis] that God must be equally capable of doing good or evil, if his action is to be called free) but in absolute spontaneity. The latter is at risk only with predeterminism, where the determining ground of an action lies in *antecedent* time, so that the action is no longer in *my* power but in the hands of nature, which determines me

---

[62] One question to ask here is how Kant can consistently hold onto (1) the thesis that freedom cannot be defined in terms of liberty of indifference, and (2) the thesis that at the noumenal level we are free to adopt a good or an evil disposition. The latter claim seems to imply that transcendental freedom is constituted, in part, by leeway freedom: the freedom either to place the moral law above self-love or to place self-love above the moral law. On this picture, noumenal "choice" (*Willkür*) will be a two-way power, an ability to choose the moral law and an ability to choose otherwise (in privileging self-love). It is odd, then, that Kant's argument in the *Metaphysics of Morals* is that leeway freedom or indifference is only an *appearance* in the phenomenal order of appearances, since in the *Religion* he seems to ascribe such freedom to the *intelligible character* of the will as such. In reply, I want to point out that Kant nowhere characterizes the noumenal choice of dispositions in terms of leeway freedom. Examined more closely, his line of reasoning reflects an *ideal of ultimate responsibility* for all of our actions, an ideal that he uses in the *Religion* to undermine "moral latitudinarianism," that is, the view that human beings are partly good and partly evil. All I take Kant to be saying in the *Religion* is that because evil is a fact, it must have its ground in our freedom, and hence we must ascribe responsibility for the evil we see in the world by locating it in our (mis)use of freedom. Beyond that, he is not making any further inference that the *constitution* of noumenal choice is a leeway power, for that would violate what he believes we can say about our freedom (as it is disclosed to us through our consciousness of the moral law). One might wonder if the emphasis I am placing on the *ascription* of ultimate responsibility for evil makes the idea "prescriptive" rather than "descriptive," as Irene McMullin (2013) argues. I find McMullin's reading compelling, as well as the hints made in this direction by George di Giovanni (2005, 193), though limitations of space prevent me from offering further argument. For a critical assessment of the prescriptive reading, see Papish 2018, 136–138.

irresistibly; since in God no temporal sequence is thinkable, this difficulty
has no place. (RGV, AA 6:50 n)

Since the topic here concerns God, many commentators have left this
passage aside in discussing Kant's theory of freedom.[63] Yet on closer
inspection we can see that Kant is making a strong statement not just about
God's freedom but about freedom as such. To frame his point, he even uses
a neologism from the recent *Freiheitsstreit*, "indeterminism." Regarding the
divine being, Kant is clear that God is not subject to a natural series of time
determinations, and so there is no problem in reconciling the concept of
freedom with God's status as a necessary being. In the course of offering this
clarification, Kant makes two claims: (1) freedom as such does not consist in
leeway indeterminism or in the multidirectional power to choose between
good and evil; and (2) freedom as such consists of absolute spontaneity. The
latter claim is under threat only from the standpoint of natural causality, in
which everything that happens is preceded in time by antecedent states. This
is why, for Kant, the only way to "save freedom" is to deny that appearances
are things-in-themselves (see A536/B564; KrV, AA 5:101).[64] As Kant
repeatedly says, without the doctrine of transcendental idealism, freedom
is "destroyed."

In hindsight, it may have been the confusion caused by the *Freiheitsstreit* that
led Kant to write the following in the late 1790s: "Freedom of choice cannot be
defined – as some have tried to define it – as the ability to make a choice for or
against the law (*libertas indifferentiae*), even though choice as a phenomenon
provides frequent examples of this in experience" (MS, AA 6:226). Whether he
was referring to Reinhold, Crusius, or some other proponent of moral libertarianism, there is no question that Kant wanted to distance himself from this

---

[63] One noteworthy exception is Derk Pereboom (2006), who (after citing RGV, AA 6:50 n) writes:
"This suggests that transcendental freedom does not essentially involve the ability to do
otherwise. Kant would seem to be a *source* rather than a *leeway* incompatibilist, stressing that
the key notion of freedom is not the ability to do otherwise, but rather being the undetermined
source of one's actions" (542). However, Pereboom goes on to say that "it is of great significance
for Kant that we human beings have the ability to do otherwise, since this is a necessary condition
for 'ought' principles applying to us" (543). But if the argument of this Element is correct, there
is no need to think that the ability to do otherwise is a necessary condition for "ought" principles
(also *pace* Korsgaard 2008). The moral "ought" implies that I *can* determine my power of choice
according to the moral law, independent of all sensible inclination, but it does not imply that
I have a genuine power to gainsay that law. Using Kohl's (2015a, 353) terms, "ought" implies
moral *ability* and an immoral *option*, where the latter refers to the corruption of choice, not its
law-governed power.

[64] As Kant writes, if appearances "are things in themselves, then freedom cannot be saved" (A536/
B564). And again: "If a human being's actions insofar as they belong to his determinations in
time were determinations of him not merely as appearance but as a thing in itself, freedom could
not be saved" (KrV, AA 5:101).

view.[65] Defining freedom as a power to choose otherwise invites the objection that the will's activity reduces to mere chance, as there will then be no rule or law that could explain why the will acts one way rather than the other. Kant does not have to contend with the Objection from Chance, I have argued, because he consistently upholds source freedom and moral necessity. The main challenge facing Kant's theory of freedom is rather the Objection from Necessity: that his theory reduces the will's activity to noumenal determinism. However, this objection can be avoided when we distinguish between heteronomous and autonomous causality. Freedom of will is a genuine power, and the moral law is the causal law of this power. Any misuse of this power is, as Kant says, not an ability, but an inability.

---

[65] For a rejoinder, see Reinhold's 1797 "Einige Bemerkungen über die in der Einleitung zu den metaphysischen Anfangsgründen der Rechtslehre von I. Kant aufgestellten Begriffe von der Freyheit."

Appendix A: Moral Progress and Perfection

As we have seen in this Element, one source of skepticism about moral necessitarianism is the worry that it reduces the will's activity to a new kind of causal necessity at the noumenal level (the Objection from Necessity). I have proposed that transcendental idealism gives us the resources to make a principled distinction between natural necessitation (relating to phenomena) and practical necessitation (relating to noumena), and that this distinction disarms the objection so formulated.[1] In this way, we can concede to the skeptic that moral necessitarianism makes the will's activity subject to a new kind of causal necessity, with the qualification that this is the autonomous causality (or *a*-causality) of a self-legislating will. As I have argued, because skepticism about moral necessitarianism comes from the thought that all causality is of a natural (or heteronomous) kind, it amounts to what Kant would call "physiocracy" – what we would today call "naturalism" – given that it illicitly restricts the category of cause and effect to the realm of appearances.

In this first Appendix, I want to address a pair of related objections facing Kant's doctrine:

Objection 1. Moral necessitarianism cannot account for moral imperfection

The argument here is that if the moral law is the causal law of a free will, then any willed violation of the moral law is not free. We have encountered a version of this argument in the work of Reinhold, who claims that defining freedom in terms of its subjection to the moral law renders the imputation of evil to an agent impossible. Answering the more general version of the worry under consideration will still be instructive, as it will help to clarify what is misguided about Reinhold's worry.

By way of reply, let me raise two points of clarification. First, on closer scrutiny we can see that the objection rests on a tacit inference from (1) the function of the moral law as the causal law of a free will (*Wille*) to (2) the idea of

---

[1] Without the resources of transcendental idealism or something similar, we have no grounds for distinguishing the lawfulness of freedom otherwise than in terms of natural causality, in which case the only room left over for freedom seems to lie in the elusive ability to do otherwise. That is more or less the dialectic of much of the contemporary literature on free will, which is why many incompatibilists defend some form of leeway freedom or liberty of indifference. From the standpoint of Kant's philosophy, however, this is a false dialectic, for the distinction between phenomena and noumena allows us to separate heteronomous from autonomous causality and align the will's activity with the latter. Kant can thereby remain a strong *incompatibilist* in denying that natural causality rules all domains of activity, while affirming that the moral law is the *causal law* of a free will.

total conformity between the moral law and the agent's power of choice (*Willkür*). But this inference is unfounded, since the doctrine of moral necessitarianism does not require the kind of freedom Kant reserves for the idea of a holy will, namely, perfect freedom. To claim that the moral law is the causal law of a free will entails only that whenever a person acts freely she does so under the principle of autonomy (without which she would not be "effective at all"). The doctrine does *not* make the further claim that whenever a person acts freely she does so in complete agreement with the principle of autonomy. That would be true of a holy will (as an ideal), whose power of choice exhibits perfect freedom, but it is not true for beings like us, who only ever act in ways that *approximate* this ideal. Moral necessitarianism does not rule out imperfect freedom, which we clearly possess, since we do approach agreement with the principle of autonomy by *degrees*.

Second, it bears repeating that Kant's doctrine of moral necessitarianism does not entail that culpable misuse of one's power of choice is impossible. To say that the moral law is the causal law of a free will does not mean that a misuse of our freedom can never occur: we can misuse our freedom in the form of frailty, impurity, or self-conceit, three degrees of the "propensity to evil" which I suggested earlier are degrees of the will's *corruptio* or *defectus* – its internal diminishment and disempowerment. Such forms of imperfection are possible from the standpoint of moral necessitarianism. All Kant is committed to saying is that evil amounts to culpable self-disempowerment – the possibility of doing evil is *not* a power or ability (*Vermögen*), since a power or ability of any kind must be law-governed. This is why Kant is committed to rejecting the concept of a diabolical will, since there is no law or principle by which one can choose evil for its own sake. As readers of the *Religion* know, Kant believes that evil always amounts to a twisting or distorting of one's original predisposition to the good, but never to the uprooting of goodness as such.

These two points of clarification are relevant, I think, for addressing a related objection to Kant's doctrine:

Objection 2. Moral necessitarianism cannot account for moral perfection

The worry here is that if the moral law is the causal law of a free will, then progress in becoming good is impossible. In many ways this is the inverse of the worry considered, but it brings a new challenge to the table. The worry of the first objection was that culpable moral imperfection is not possible from the standpoint of moral necessitarianism; the worry now is that, given this doctrine, we lose any basis to explain how degrees of approximation to morally good action are possible, without which we cannot make sense of the idea of improvement along the path of becoming good.

As before, I want to address this concern by clarifying two points. The first is that from the standpoint of transcendental idealism, talk of improvement, progress, and perfection pertains to the domain of explanation subject to time determinations: the phenomenal realm of things as they appear. There is no basis for extending the representations of *before* and *after* to the noumenal realm of things-in-themselves, since that domain is not subject to time determinations at all. Without getting detained by the intricacies of Kant's version of idealism, all I want to emphasize here is that Kant is committed to saying that we inhabit both "worlds" or "standpoints" *simultaneously*[2] and that we can understand our path to becoming good in time as an endless series whose ground is an expression of our noumenal character. Regardless of how we understand the metaphysics of Kant's idealism, the relevant point is that *degrees* of approximation to morality are possible when we specify where this approximation occurs – namely, at the phenomenal level – and where the idea of its perfection lies – namely, at the noumenal level. Instead of ruling out the idea of becoming good, then, Kant's idealism gives us the resources needed to explain the very possibility of becoming good.[3]

What these resources also bring to light is that Kant's moral necessitarianism does a better job of explaining moral perfection than its rival theory, liberty of indifference. As we have just seen, to say that the moral law is the causal law of a free will does not entail that our power of choice is perfect. All the doctrine states is that whenever we exercise our power of choice, the moral law is the effective principle of our willing. From the standpoint of the sensible world, the way we bring ourselves into harmony with this principle admits of infinite degrees, since the idea of its total perfection cannot be restricted to any condition of time. For imperfect beings like ourselves, the moral law presents us with an *endless task* – the task of becoming fully autonomous. Yet it is not clear that the idea of moral improvement has any place within a framework of liberty of indifference, since the total perfection of a leeway power would amount to something like pure arbitrariness or pure randomness of choice, which would be quite strange to say the least. From the standpoint of Kant's philosophy, that is not an *ideal* of freedom. It is, rather, an absurdity, a nonentity, an *Unding*.

---

[2] See, for instance, GMS, AA 4:454, which I discuss in Ware 2021.
[3] This still leaves open the question of what kind of idealism is suited to accomplishing this task – a merely *epistemological* version or a stronger, *metaphysical* one? I agree with Lucy Allais (2015, 305) that "it is hard to see how [the former] explains the possibility of freedom as an alternative kind of causality," though I am not sure that the latter "makes freedom utterly mysterious." For a fruitful start to this much-needed conversation, see Jauernig 2021, esp. chap. 5.

Appendix B: Timeline of the Freedom Controversy

The 1780s and 1790s were exciting times for those who enjoyed intellectual Quarrels. There was the *Pantheismusstreit* (pantheism controversy), ignited by Lessing's alleged confession of Spinozism, a controversy that drew in all the luminaries of Germany at the time; there was the *Atheismusstreit* (atheism controversy), which led to the infamous expulsion of Fichte from his Chair of Philosophy at the University of Jena; and there was what I have called the *Freiheitsstreit* (freedom controversy) between Kant and his early critics. This last controversy began in 1788 and reached its climax in 1793, but its aftermath continued well into the nineteenth century. Below is a timeline of the central publications covered in this Element.

1781   Immanuel Kant, *Critique of Pure Reason*, first edition
1785   Kant, *Groundwork for the Metaphysics of Morals*
1788   Kant, *Critique of Practical Reason*
1788   Johann August Heinrich Ulrich, *Eleutheriology, or Concerning Freedom and Necessity*
1789   Karl Leonhard Reinhold, *Attempt at a New Theory of the Human Power of Representation*
1790   Carl Christian Erhard Schmid, *Attempt at a Moral Philosophy*, first edition
1792   Kant, "On the Radical Evil of Human Nature," in the April issue of the *Berlinische Monatsschrift*
1792   Reinhold, *Letters on Kantian Philosophy*, second volume
1792   Salomon Maimon, letter to Kant, November 30, 1792
1793   Maimon, *Quarrels in the Field of Philosophy*
1793   Christoph Andreas Leonhard Creuzer, *Skeptical Observations on Freedom of the Will*
1793   Kant, *Religion within the Bounds of Mere Reason*
1793   Johann Gottlieb Fichte, review of Creuzer, in the October issue of the *Allgemeine Literatur-Zeitung*
1797   Kant, *Metaphysics of Morals*

Abbreviations

With the exception of the *Critique of Pure Reason*, cited according to its standard pagination (A = 1st ed., 1781; B = 2nd ed., 1787), Kant's published works are cited according to the abbreviations below, by volume and page in the Akademieausgabe (AA = Kant 1902–). His unpublished *Reflexionen* are cited by number. Translation decisions are my own, although I have consulted and sometimes followed the Cambridge translations edited by Paul Guyer and Allen Wood (Kant 1992–).

FM	*What Real Progress Has Metaphysics Made in Germany since the Time of Leibniz and Wolff?*
GMS	*Groundwork for the Metaphysics of Morals*
KpV	*Critique of Practical Reason*
KrV	*Critique of Pure Reason*
KU	*Critique of the Power of Judgment*
MS	*Metaphysics of Morals*
PND	*New Elucidation of the First Principles of Metaphysical Cognition*
Prol	*Prolegomena to Any Future Metaphysics*
Refl	*Reflexionen*
RGV	*Religion within the Boundaries of Mere Reason*
VAMS	*Preparatory Work on the Metaphysics of Morals*
V-Met/Dohna	*Metaphysik-Dohna*
V-Mo/Mron II	*Lectures Mrongovius*

References

Abaci, Uygar. 2022. "Noumenal Freedom and Kant's Modal Antinomy." *Kantian Review* 27, no. 2: 175–194.

Alderwick, Charlotte. 2021. *Schelling's Ontology of Powers.* Edinburgh: Edinburgh University Press.

Allais, Lucy. 2015. *Manifest Reality: Kant's Idealism and His Realism.* Oxford: Oxford University Press.

Allison, Henry. 1990. *Kant's Theory of Freedom.* Cambridge: Cambridge University Press.

2020. *Kant's Conception of Freedom.* Cambridge: Cambridge University Press.

Ameriks, Karl. 2000. *Kant and the Fate of Autonomy.* Cambridge: Cambridge University Press.

2003. "On Two Non-Realist Interpretations of Kant's Ethics." In *Interpreting Kant's Critiques,* 262–281. Oxford: Oxford University Press.

2012. *Kant's Elliptical Path.* Oxford: Oxford University Press.

Anselm. (1080–1086) 2007. *De libertate arbitrii (On Freedom of Choice).* In *Anselm: Basic Writings,* edited and translated by Thomas Williams, 145–165. Indianapolis: Hackett.

Augustine. 2010. *On the Free Choice of the Will, On Grace and Free Choice, and Other Writings,* edited and translated by Peter King. Cambridge: Cambridge University Press.

Aylsworth, Timothy. 2020. "Bolstering the Keystone: Kant on the Incomprehensibility of Freedom." *Archiv für Geschichte der Philosophie* 102, no. 2: 261–298.

Bojanowski, Jochen. 2012. "Ist Kant ein Kompatibilist?" In *Sind wir Bürger zweier Welten? Freiheit und moralische Verantwortung im transzendentalen Idealismus,* edited by Mario Brandhorst, Andree Hahmann, and Bernd Ludwig, 59–76. Leipzig: Meiner.

Creuzer, Leonhard. 1793. *Skeptische Betrachtungen über die Freyheit des Willens mit Hinsicht auf die neuesten Theorien über dieselbe.* Jena: Croker.

Crusius, Christian August. (1744) 1969. *Anweisung, vernünftig zu leben, darinnen nach Erklärung der Natur des menschlichen Willens, die natürlichen Pflichten und allgemeinen Klugheitslehren im richtigen Zusammenhange vorgetragen werden.* Vol. 1 of *Die philosophischen Hauptwerke,* edited by Giorgio Tonelli. Hildesheim: Olms.

De Boer, Karin. 2020. *Kant's Reform of Metaphysics: The Critique of Pure Reason Reconsidered.* Cambridge: Cambridge University Press.

Descartes, René. (1641) 1996. *Meditations on First Philosophy*, translated by John Cottingham. Cambridge: Cambridge University Press.

Di Giovanni, George. 2005. *Freedom and Religion in Kant and His Immediate Successors: The Vocation of Humankind, 1774–1800*. Cambridge: Cambridge University Press.

Dunn, Nicholas. 2015. "A Lawful Freedom: Kant's Practical Refutation of Noumenal Chance." *Kant Studies Online* 1: 149–177.

Dyck, Corey W. 2016. "Spontaneity *before* the Critical Turn: The Spontaneity of the Mind in Crusius, the Pre-Critical Kant, and Tetens." *Journal of the History of Philosophy* 54, no. 4: 625–648.

Forthcoming. "Power, Harmony, and Freedom: Debating Causation in 18th Century Germany." In *The Oxford Handbook of Eighteenth Century German Philosophy*, edited by Frederick Beiser and Brandon Look. Oxford: Oxford University Press.

Engstrom, Stephen. 2009. *The Form of Practical Knowledge: A Study of the Categorical Imperative*. Cambridge, MA: Harvard University Press.

Fabbianelli, Faustino. 2015. "Kant's Concept of Moral *imputatio*." In *Reading Kant's Lectures*, edited by Robert R. Clewis, 200–220. Berlin: De Gruyter.

Fichte, Johann Gottlieb. (1793) 1846. Review of *Skeptische Betrachtungen über die Freyheit des Willens mit Hinsicht auf die neuesten Theorien über dieselbe*, by Leonhard Creuzer. In *Johann Gottlieb Fichtes sämmtliche Werke*, edited by I. H. Fichte, vol. 8, 411–417. Berlin: Veit.

Fischer, John Martin. 2011. *Deep Control: Essays on Free Will and Value*. Oxford: Oxford University Press.

Frankfurt, Harry. 1969. "Alternate Possibilities and Moral Responsibility." *Journal of Philosophy* 66, no. 23: 829–839.

Franklin, Christopher Evan. 2011. "Farewell to the Luck (and Mind) Argument." *Philosophical Studies* 156, no. 2: 199–230.

Frierson, Patrick R. 2014. *Kant's Empirical Psychology*. Cambridge: Cambridge University Press.

Gardner, Sebastian. 2017. "The Metaphysics of Human Freedom: From Kant's Transcendental Idealism to Schelling's *Freiheitsschrift*." *British Journal for the History of Philosophy* 25, no. 1: 133–156.

Grenberg, Jeanine. 2009. "Social Dimensions of Kant's Concept of Radical Evil." In *Kant's Anatomy of Evil*, edited by Sharon Anderson-Gold and Pablo Muchnik, 173–213. Cambridge: Cambridge University Press.

Guyer, Paul. 2009. "Problems with Freedom: Kant's Argument in *Groundwork* III and Its Subsequent Emendations." In *Kant's Groundwork of the Metaphysics of Morals: A Critical Guide*, edited by Jens Timmermann, 176–202. Cambridge: Cambridge University Press.

2017. "The Struggle for Freedom: Freedom of Will in Kant and Reinhold." In *Kant on Persons and Agency*, edited by Eric Watkins, 120–137. Cambridge: Cambridge University Press.

Hoffmann, Tobias. 2019. "Freedom without Choice: Medieval Theories of the Essence of Freedom." In *The Cambridge Companion to Medieval Ethics*, edited by Thomas Williams, 194–216. Cambridge: Cambridge University Press.

2021. *Free Will and the Rebel Angels in Medieval Philosophy*. Cambridge: Cambridge University Press.

Hogan, Desmond. 2009a. "Noumenal Affection." *The Philosophical Review* 118, no. 4: 501–532.

2009b. "Three Kinds of Rationalism and the Non-Spatiality of Things in Themselves." *Journal of the History of Philosophy* 47, no. 3: 355–382.

Insole, Christopher J. 2013. *Kant and the Creation of Freedom: A Theological Problem*. Oxford: Oxford University Press.

Jacobi, Friedrich Heinrich. 1785. *Über die Lehre des Spinoza in Briefen an den Herrn Moses Mendelssohn*. Breslau: Löwe.

Jauernig, Anja. 2021. *The World According to Kant: Appearances and Things in Themselves in Critical Idealism*. Oxford: Oxford University Press.

Kain, Patrick. 2021. "The Development of Kant's Conception of Divine Freedom." In *Kant and Leibniz*, edited by Brandon C. Look, 295–319. Oxford: Oxford University Press.

Kant, Immanuel. 1902–. *Gesammelte Schriften*. Edited by Preussischen Akademie der Wissenschaften (vols. 1–22), Deutschen Akademie der Wissenschaften zu Berlin (vol. 23), and Akademie der Wissenschaften zu Göttingen (vol. 24–). 29 vols. Berlin: De Gruyter.

1992–. *The Cambridge Edition of the Works of Immanuel Kant*. General editors Paul Guyer and Allen W. Wood. Cambridge: Cambridge University Press.

Kemp, Ryan, and Christopher Iacovetti. 2020. *Reason and Conversion in Kierkegaard and the German Idealists*. London: Routledge.

Khurana, Thomas. 2011. "Einteilung." In *Paradoxien der Autonomie: Freiheit und Gesetz I*, edited by Thomas Khurana and Christoph Menke, 7–23. Berlin: August.

Khurana, Thomas, and Christoph Menke, eds. 2011. *Paradoxien der Autonomie: Freiheit und Gesetz I*. Berlin: August

Kim, Halla. 2015. *Kant and the Foundations of Morality*. New York: Rowman & Littlefield.

Kohl, Markus. 2015a. "Kant on Determinism and the Categorical Imperative." *Ethics* 125, no. 2: 331–356.

2015b. "Kant on Freedom of Empirical Thought." *Journal of the History of Philosophy* 53, no. 2: 301–326.

Korsgaard, Christine M. 1996. "Morality as Freedom." In *Creating the Kingdom of Ends*, 159–187. Cambridge: Cambridge University Press.

2008. "The Normativity of Instrumental Reason." In *The Constitution of Agency: Essays on Practical Reason and Moral Psychology*, 27–68. Oxford: Oxford University Press.

2009. *Self-Constitution: Agency, Identity, and Integrity*. Oxford: Oxford University Press.

Leibniz, Gottfried Wilhelm, and Samuel Clarke. (1715) 2000. *Correspondence*, edited and translated by Roger Ariew. Indianapolis: Hackett.

Maimon, Salomon. 1793. *Streifereien im Gebiete der Philosophie*. Vol. 1. Berlin: Wilhelm Vieweg.

Martin, Wayne. 2018. "Fichte's Creuzer Review and the Transformation of the Free Will Problem." *European Journal of Philosophy* 26, no. 2: 717–729.

McCarty, Richard. 2008. "Kant's Incorporation Requirement: Freedom and Character in the Empirical World." *Canadian Journal of Philosophy* 38, no. 3: 425–451.

2009. *Kant's Theory of Action*. Oxford: Oxford University Press.

McClear, Colin. 2020. "On the Transcendental Freedom of the Intellect." *Ergo: An Open Access Journal of Philosophy* 7, no. 2: 35–104. https://doi.org/10.3998/ergo.12405314.0007.002.

McMullin, Irene. 2013. "Kant on Radical Evil and the Origin of Moral Responsibility." *Kantian Review* 18, no. 1: 49–72.

Merritt, Melissa. 2021. "Nature, Corruption, and Freedom: Stoic Ethics in Kant's *Religion*." *European Journal of Philosophy* 29, no. 1: 3–24.

Morrisson, Iain P. D. 2008. *Kant and the Role of Pleasure in Moral Action*. Athens: Ohio University Press.

Noller, Jörg. 2018. "Vom Unvermögen zum Un-Vermögen: Reinhold und Schelling über unmoralische Freiheit nach Kant." *Deutsche Zeitschrift für Philosophie* 66, no. 2: 162–182.

2019. "'Practical Reason Is Not the Will': Kant and Reinhold's Dilemma." *European Journal of Philosophy* 27, no. 4: 852–864.

Papish, Laura. 2018. *Kant on Evil, Self-Deception, and Moral Reform*. Oxford: Oxford University Press.

Pereboom, Derk. 2001. *Living without Free Will*. Cambridge: Cambridge University Press.

2006. "Kant on Transcendental Freedom." *Philosophy and Phenomenological Research* 73, no. 3: 537–567.

Reinhold, Karl Leonhard. 1789. *Versuch einer neuen Theorie des menschlichen Vorstellungsvermögens*. Jena: Croker.

1792. *Briefe über die Kantische Philosophie*. Vol. 2. Leipzig: Goschen.

(1797) 1975. "Einige Bemerkungen über die in der Einleitung zu den metaphysischen Anfangsgründen der Rechtslehre von I. Kant aufgestellten Begriffe von der Freyheit." In *Materialien zu Kants Kritik der praktischen Vernunft*, edited by Rüdiger Bittner and Konrad Cramer, 310–324. Frankfurt am Main: Suhrkamp.

Roehr, Sabine. 2003. "Freedom and Autonomy in Schiller." *Journal of the History of Ideas* 64, no. 1: 119–134.

Russell, Francey. 2020. "Kantian Self-Conceit and the Two Guises of Authority." *Canadian Journal of Philosophy* 50, no. 2: 268–283.

Russell, Paul. 2017. "Sorabji and the Dilemma of Determinism." In *The Limits of Free Will*, 3–10. New York: Oxford University Press.

Saunders, Joe. 2016. "Kant and the Problem of Recognition: Freedom, Transcendental Idealism, and the Third-Person." *International Journal of Philosophical Studies* 24, no. 2: 164–182.

2019. "Kant and Degrees of Responsibility." *Journal of Applied Philosophy* 36, no. 1: 137–154.

Scanlan, James P. 1999. "The Case against Rational Egoism in Dostoevsky's *Notes from Underground*." *Journal of the History of Ideas* 60, no. 3: 549–567.

Schafer, Karl. Forthcoming. "Practical Cognition and Knowledge of Things-in-Themselves." In *The Idea of Freedom: New Essays on the Kantian Theory of Freedom*, edited by Evan Tiffany and Dai Heide. Oxford: Oxford University Press.

Schmid, Carl Christian Erhard. (1790) 1792. *Versuch einer Moralphilosophie*. Jena: Croker.

Sensen, Oliver. 2011. *Kant on Human Dignity*. Berlin: De Gruyter.

Shabo, Seth. 2020. "The Two-Stage Luck Objection." *Noûs* 54, no. 1: 3–23.

Smith, Daniel J. 2021. "An Ethics of Temptation: Schelling's Contribution to the Freedom Controversy." *European Journal of Philosophy* 29, no. 4: 731–745.

Stang, Nicholas F. 2016. *Kant's Modal Metaphysics*. Oxford: Oxford University Press.

Stern, Robert. 2011. *Understanding Moral Obligation: Kant, Hegel, Kierkegaard*. Cambridge: Cambridge University Press.

Sticker, Martin. 2021. *Rationalizing (*Vernünfteln*)*. Cambridge: Cambridge University Press.

Tenenbaum, Sergio. 2007. *Appearances of the Good: An Essay on the Nature of Practical Reason*. Cambridge: Cambridge University Press.

2021. "Duality of Motivation and the Guise of the Good in Kant's Practical Philosophy." *Philosophical Explorations* 24, no. 1: 75–92.

Timmermann, Jens. 2003. *Sittengesetz und Freiheit: Untersuchungen zu Immanuel Kants Theorie des freien Willens*. Berlin: De Gruyter.

Tizzard, Jessica. 2021. "Kantian Moral Psychology and Weakness." *Philosophers' Imprint* 21, no. 16: 1–28. http://hdl.handle.net/2027/spo.3521354.0021.016.

Tognazzini, Neal A. 2015. "Grounding the Luck Objection." *Australasian Journal of Philosophy* 93, no. 1: 127–138.

Tolley, Clinton. 2006. "Kant on the Nature of Logical Laws." *Philosophical Topics* 34, nos. 1–2: 371–407.

Ulrich, Johann August Heinrich. 1788. *Eleutheriologie, oder über Freyheit und Nothwendigkeit*. Jena: Croker.

Walschots, Michael H. 2021. "Crusius on Freedom of the Will." In *Christian August Crusius (1715–1775): Philosophy between Reason and Revelation*, edited by Frank Grunert, Andree Hahmann, and Gideon Stiening, 189–208. Berlin: De Gruyter.

Walsh, John. 2020. "The Fact of Freedom: Reinhold's Theory of Free Will Reconsidered." In *The Concept of Will in Classical German Philosophy: Between Ethics, Politics, and Metaphysics*, edited by Manja Kisner and Jörg Noller, 89–104. Berlin: De Gruyter.

Ware, Owen. 2014. "Rethinking Kant's Fact of Reason." *Philosophers' Imprint* 14, no. 32: 1–21. http://hdl.handle.net/2027/spo.3521354.0014.032.

2015. "Agency and Evil in Fichte's Ethics." *Philosophers' Imprint* 15, no. 11: 1–21. http://hdl.handle.net/2027/spo.3521354.0015.011

2017. "Kant's Deductions of Morality and Freedom." *Canadian Journal of Philosophy* 47, no. 1: 116–147.

2020. *Fichte's Moral Philosophy*. New York: Oxford University Press.

2021. *Kant's Justification of Ethics*. Oxford: Oxford University Press.

2023. "Kant and the Fate of Freedom: 1788–1800." In *Freedom after Kant: From German Idealism to Ethics and the Self*, edited by Joe Saunders, 45–62. London: Bloomsbury.

Watkins, Eric. 2004. *Kant and the Metaphysics of Causality*. Cambridge: Cambridge University Press.

2019. *Kant on Laws*. Cambridge: Cambridge University Press.

Willaschek, Marcus. 2017. "Freedom as a Postulate." In *Kant on Persons and Agency*, edited by Eric Watkins, 101–119. Cambridge: Cambridge University Press.

Wood, Allen W. 1984. "Kant's Compatibilism." In *Self and Nature in Kant's Philosophy*, edited by Allen W. Wood, 73–101. Ithaca: Cornell University Press.

1999. *Kant's Ethical Thought*. Cambridge: Cambridge University Press.

Acknowledgments

For helpful input on earlier drafts of this Element, I am grateful to Lucy Allais, Timothy Aylsworth, Anthony Bruno, Ian Drummond, Nicholas Dunn, Pat Kain, Joe Saunders, Robert Stern, Martin Sticker, John Walsh, Eric Watkins, and Ryan Wines. I have also benefited from (written or spoken) exchanges on this topic with Uygar Abaci, Karl Ameriks, Tarek Dika, Corey Dyck, Dai Heide, Markus Kohl, Christine Korsgaard, Martin Pickavé, Sergio Tenenbaum, Evan Tiffany, and Clinton Tolley, and with students at Temple University (2011–2014), Simon Fraser University (2014–2017), and the University of Toronto (2017–present). I was fortunate to have the opportunity to present my ideas in this Element at Karin de Boer's Leuven Seminar in Classical German Philosophy (October 27, 2022), and I am thankful to the organizers and participants of the Seminar, especially Paul Guyer, who served as my respondent that day. Lastly, many thanks to the editors of the Cambridge Elements series on Kant – Desmond Hogan, Howard Williams, Allen Wood, and their anonymous reviewer – for constructive feedback and encouragement. Research for this publication was supported by the Social Sciences and Humanities Research Council of Canada in the form of an Insight Grant.

Cambridge Elements ⹀

The Philosophy of Immanuel Kant

Desmond Hogan
Princeton University
Desmond Hogan joined the philosophy department at Princeton in 2004. His interests include Kant, Leibniz and German rationalism, early modern philosophy, and questions about causation and freedom. Recent work includes 'Kant on the Foreknowledge of Contingent Truths', *Res Philosophica* 91 (1) (2014); 'Kant's Theory of Divine and Secondary Causation', in Brandon Look (ed.) *Leibniz and Kant*, Oxford University Press (2021); 'Kant and the Character of Mathematical Inference', in Carl Posy and Ofra Rechter (eds.) *Kant's Philosophy of Mathematics Vol. I*, Cambridge University Press (2020).

Howard Williams
University of Cardiff
Howard Williams was appointed Honorary Distinguished Professor at the Department of Politics and International Relations, University of Cardiff in 2014. He is also Emeritus Professor in Political Theory at the Department of International Politics, Aberystwyth University, a member of the Coleg Cymraeg Cenedlaethol (Welsh-language national college) and a Fellow of the Learned Society of Wales. He is the author of *Marx* (1980); *Kant's Political Philosophy* (1983); *Concepts of Ideology* (1988); *Hegel, Heraclitus and Marx's Dialectic* (1989); *International Relations in Political Theory* (1992); *International Relations and the Limits of Political Theory* (1996); *Kant's Critique of Hobbes: Sovereignty and Cosmopolitanism* (2003); *Kant and the End of War* (2012) and is currently editor of the journal Kantian Review. He is writing a book on the Kantian legacy in political philosophy for a new series edited by Paul Guyer.

Allen Wood
Indiana University
Allen Wood is Ward W. and Priscilla B. Woods Professor Emeritus at Stanford University. He was a John S. Guggenheim Fellow at the Free University in Berlin, a National Endowment for the Humanities Fellow at the University of Bonn and Isaiah Berlin Visiting Professor at the University of Oxford. He is on the editorial board of eight philosophy journals, five book series and The Stanford Encyclopedia of Philosophy. Along with Paul Guyer, Professor Wood is co-editor of The Cambridge Edition of the Works of Immanuel Kant and translator of the Critique of Pure Reason. He is the author or editor of a number of other works, mainly on Kant, Hegel and Karl Marx. His most recently published books are *Fichte's Ethical Thought*, Oxford University Press (2016) and *Kant and Religion*, Cambridge University Press (2020). Wood is a member of the American Academy of Arts and Sciences.

About the Series
This Cambridge Elements series provides an extensive overview of Kant's philosophy and its impact upon philosophy and philosophers. Distinguished Kant specialists provide an up-to-date summary of the results of current research in their fields and give their own take on what they believe are the most significant debates influencing research, drawing original conclusions.

Cambridge Elements ☰

The Philosophy of Immanuel Kant

Elements in the Series

The Guarantee of Perpetual Peace
Wolfgang Ertl

Kant and Global Distributive Justice
Sylvie Loriaux

Anthropology from a Kantian Point of View
Robert B. Louden

Introducing Kant's Critique of Pure Reason
Paul Guyer and Allen Wood

Kant's Theory of Conscience
Samuel Kahn

Rationalizing (Vernünfteln)
Martin Sticker

Kant and the French Revolution
Reidar Maliks

The Kantian Federation
Luigi Caranti

The Politics of Beauty: A Study of Kant's Critique of Taste
Susan Meld Shell

Kant's Theory of Labour
Jordan Pascoe

Kant's Late Philosophy of Nature: The Opus postumum
Stephen Howard

Kant on Freedom
Owen Ware

A full series listing is available at: www.cambridge.org/EPIK

Printed in the United States
by Baker & Taylor Publisher Services